In this book, Anthony C[...] of the book of Jonah, de[...] abounds in love and grace [...] every Christian who wants to gain a bigger heart for the nations and a better grasp of the sovereignty of God, the patience of God, the grace of God, and the gospel of God, which is the power of God to salvation to everyone who believes.

Burk Parsons, senior pastor of Saint Andrew's Chapel and editor of *Tabletalk* magazine

We may run from mercy, but mercy runs after us nonetheless. Tony's pastoral heart and prophetic preaching voice are on full display in this look at the story of Jonah. You can hear his voice as you read it. Tony's hard-won wisdom and application of principles to our struggle with sin are incredibly relevant to our daily lives. Share this book with someone you know.

Wendy Alsup, author of *Practical Theology for Women: How Knowing God Makes a Difference in Our Daily Lives* and *Is the Bible Good for Women? Seeking Clarity and Confidence through a Jesus-Centered Understanding of Scripture*

As a pastor, I read commentaries every week. Written with the heart, wisdom, and skill of a seasoned shepherd, *Running from Mercy* will help both pastor and Bible teacher translate the truths from Jonah into convicting messages. Please get a copy of Pastor Carter's work. He'll make sure you're ready to teach/preach the book of Jonah on Sunday.

Bobby Scott, co-pastor of Community of Faith Bible Church

A timely word from an old book through a wise pastor. In *Running from Mercy*, Anthony Carter helps us understand the text, how it relates to us, and most important the gracious, merciful, and awesome God the book of Jonah is ultimately about. Grateful for Carter's work and you will be too!

Trillia Newbell, author of *God's Very Good Idea, Enjoy,* and *Fear and Faith*

An exceptional book! Those who read this succinctly clear exposition of the book of Jonah will be tremendously encouraged. Carter offers a fresh perspective on Jonah. We often make much of the characters of the Bible (in this case, Jonah), but Carter flips the script, and rightfully, so in order to place the primary focus on the greatness of God displayed in His mercy and grace in fulfilling His redemptive purpose. After reading, *Running from Mercy: Jonah and the Surprising Story of God's Unstoppable Grace,* I was extremely encouraged and reminded of how wonderful God's mercy was and is in pursuing those whom He loves.

Byron Johnson, founder and executive director of VISION 9:38

Yes and amen to this pithy and profound piece of gospel truth by Tony Carter! Who cannot relate to the Jonah-like tendency to run from the God we should be running for, or running to? As today's cultural winds blow and theological tides shift, it is glorious news to hear that God's grace is relentless in His pursuit of us. Carter, who has a way of making deep theological truth amazingly graspable, has provided insights and inspiration for the pulpit and the pew, for the business world and "the block." I must commend this book and testify that, as a repenting sinner, I was refueled and renewed in my affections for my Rescuer.

William Duce Branch, assistant professor of preaching at the College at Southeastern Baptist Theological Seminary

Running from Mercy

ANTHONY J. CARTER

–

Running from Mercy

JONAH *and the*

SURPRISING STORY

of GOD'S

UNSTOPPABLE

GRACE

–

B&H
PUBLISHING GROUP

NASHVILLE, TENNESSEE

978-1-5359-0245-8

Published by B&H Publishing Group
Nashville, Tennessee

Dewey Decimal Classification: 234.1
Subject Heading: JONAH, PROPHET \ GRACE
(THEOLOGY) \ GOD

Cover design by FaceOut Studio.

1 2 3 4 5 6 • 21 20 19 18

To Ralph and Patty Massullo—good friends and faithful
servants of the gospel of Jesus Christ to the nations

Contents

Preface xi

Introduction 1

1: Grace for the Rebellious (Jonah 1:1–6) 5

2: You Can't Outrun God (Jonah 1:7–16) 31

3: Divine Appointments (Jonah 1:17–2:2) 55

4: True Repentance (Jonah 2:1–10) 75

5: Redemption (Jonah 3:1–10) .97

6: Jonah's Resentment, God's Restraint (Jonah 4:1–4) . . 119

7: Our Big God (Jonah 4:5–11) 137

Conclusion: Mercy Came Running 159

Study Questions 165

Notes 171

Preface

I have had the privilege of writing several books. Every time I am reminded that I never write alone. Each time I endeavor to persevere through the task of writing a book, I find myself needing help and encouragement along the way. This time was no different. I found help in both God's Word and God's people.

Jonah has long been a particularly poignant story for me. Ever since the days of my youth, I have been drawn to the drama contained in its pages. As a youth the brevity drew me in because it was one of the few books of the Bible I could read quickly and understand. As I grew, the brevity fascinated me even more. Not because I could read it so quickly but because there was so much truth of God packed in so few words. Today I continue to marvel at Jonah because too many times in my life my testimony has been that of one running from God, only to be run down by God. Today, more than ever, I realize I am who I am by the grace of God alone. I know I am not alone in this. I wrote this book for you and me.

If you find that you are one who has questioned God's will, wondered if He was fair or if He cared, I pray this book will encourage you to trust God still. If you find that you are one who sees your sin as great and inescapable, I trust the words in these pages will show you that God is greater. And if you are one who too often thinks that circumstances in life are more than you can handle, I trust you will find encouragement to look to the God who, in Christ Jesus, is in you, your hope and glory.

Every time I read or meditate on Jonah, I am reminded that I am never alone. I hope you do too. God has given us help. He has given us one another. He has given us Himself.

There are a few people whom God particularly used to help me in completing this book.

Thanks to Joshua Mathis for his faithful service and assistance in helping this book come to print. Thanks to the elders of East Point Church, who make sure I have time to write and reflect on the things of God to share with the people of God. Thanks to Ruth Fowler, who is an administrator, friend, graphic designer, and artist. She has few words, but her service and gifts speak loudly of her love for Christ and His church.

Thanks to Taylor Combs and the team at B&H Publishing Group for believing in this project and working diligently to see it come to fruition. Thanks for your encouragement and thoughtful suggestions.

Also thanks to Adriane. God never left Jonah alone. You are an everyday reminder to me that He hasn't left me either.

Reader, I pray you find much to chew on in the pages of this book. But more important, I pray this book causes you to take another look at the book of Jonah and find much about the greatness of God's grace to chew and live on as well.

Tony Carter
East Point Church 2017

Introduction

"Call me Ishmael," is one of the most iconic beginnings to a book ever written. It begins the classic *Moby Dick* by Herman Melville. *Moby Dick* has been called the greatest American novel in history, and for good reason. When Herman Melville penned his now-famous book, I doubt he knew the literary impact and inspirational quality of his storytelling. Melville himself took much inspiration from the Bible; in particular, the biblical account of the prophet Jonah. At the heart of *Moby Dick* is a great whale. At the heart of Jonah is a great God.

"Call me Jonah," could easily be the beginning of a book on the ministry of Jonah. Jonah's story is one of the most epic in the Bible, and through the years it has been a favorite of both serious and casual Bible readers. It has served as source and inspiration for both cartoon animation and dramatic theatrical productions. Both old and young have found it insightful, instructional, and entertaining. Both Bible scholar and Sunday school student have found much to ruminate on in the short but eventful account. Still, Jonah is not without controversy.

Through the years, and even more so in modern times, the question of the reality of Jonah has been raised. Some have suggested that Jonah, rather than being a literal account of actual events, should be read and understood as a parable, much in the same vein as the prodigal son and the good Samaritan. In this understanding Jonah is a fictional story with real practical and spiritual insights, consequences, and instruction.

On the other hand, the majority report throughout the history of the church has been that Jonah was an actual prophet called by God to preach to an actual people who, along with Jonah, actually experienced the events contained in this book. Though the argument for the parabolic nature of Jonah may seem reasonable and does not necessarily take away the message of the book, the truthfulness and reality of Jonah seems well enough established for us to accept it as factual. There are several reasons for doing so.

First, Jonah is an actual person established in Scripture. We know he had a family and a father, whose name was Amittai (Jonah 1:1; 2 Kings 14:25). God had commissioned Jonah on another occasion to prophecy good news to the nation of Israel. According to 2 Kings 14:24-27, God sent Jonah with a word of mercy and grace for Israel, despite the rebellion and disobedience of King Jeroboam. Jonah prophesied that God would bless Israel, and she would experience prosperity accordingly. Consequently, Jonah's first experience as a prophet was a pleasant one. He experienced prophetic prosperity that no doubt brought him popularity and pleasure.

Second, Nineveh was a real city. There is no argument about the nature of the capitol city of the Assyrian Empire. Nineveh was a great city, as the book of Jonah says (Jonah 1:2). It was a large metropolis, just as it is written in Jonah (Jonah 3:3), with upwards of 130,000 people at its peak. What the book of Jonah says about Nineveh is accurate and gives credence to the trustworthiness of the rest of the account.

Third, in the New Testament Jesus speaks of Jonah in a way that assumes not only that His listeners were familiar with the prophet but also that Jonah's story was well known and accepted. When speaking of His death, burial, and resurrection to unbelieving persons, Jesus declared:

> For as Jonah was in the belly of the huge fish three days and three nights, so the Son of Man will be in the heart of the earth three days and three nights. The men of Nineveh will stand up at the judgment with this gener-ation and condemn it, because they repented at Jonah's preaching; and look—something greater than Jonah is here. (Matt. 12:40–41)

Jesus referred to Himself as "something greater than Jonah." This seems to imply the reality of Jonah and the literal, historical reality of his experience in the belly of the fish, just as Jesus was literally crucified, died, was buried, and was resurrected.

Moby Dick is a fictional story about a great whale. Jonah is a factual story about a great God. Yes, Jonah is about a man and a fish, a great storm, revival, and repentance. But more than all these, Jonah is about God and the unstoppable greatness of His mercy and grace. To say Jonah is about a fish is to say *Romeo and Juliet* is about a school yard crush. The great fish of Jonah is merely an instrument pointing to the greatness of God's grace, with which God pursues rebellious sinners to their everlasting delight.

Jonah is an old, old story. And yet it still offers to us insight, encouragement, and faith for living faithfully in our new world. In a world that is changing at a pace unimaginable by Jonah and his contemporaries, we can still look to the simplicity of God's dealing with Jonah to see what faith looks like in our world today. Jonah was a rebel. We are rebels too. Jonah was running. We run too. Many of us run as fast as we can away from God, but God's grace is faster.

God's grace was great to Jonah. To us God's grace is greater still.

Grace for the Rebellious
Jonah 1:1–6

———

The word of the LORD came to Jonah son of Amittai: "Get up!
Go to the great city of Nineveh and preach against it because
their evil has come up before me." Jonah got up to flee to Tarshish
from the LORD's presence. He went down to Joppa and found
a ship going to Tarshish. He paid the fare and went down into
it to go with them to Tarshish from the LORD's presence.

But the LORD threw a great wind onto the sea, and such a great storm
arose on the sea that the ship threatened to break apart. The sailors were
afraid, and each cried out to his god. They threw the ship's cargo into
the sea to lighten the load. Meanwhile, Jonah had gone down to the lowest part of the vessel and had stretched out and fallen into a deep sleep.

The captain approached him and said, "What are you doing sound asleep? Get up! Call to your god. Maybe
this god will consider us, and we won't perish."

Most of us are familiar with the name Benedict Arnold. It is a name infamously associated with the idea of treason. But what most people probably don't know about Benedict Arnold is that before he committed treason against the colonial states of America, he was a much-accomplished general in the colonial army.

As the Revolutionary War waged on, Benedict Arnold became frustrated by the way the war was progressing and offended that he did not receive the notoriety and the accolades he thought he deserved. Furthermore, he considered defeat at the hands of the British to be inevitable. Consequently, he thought he would get the jump on his comrades and get back in the good graces of the British before it was too late. So he decided to switch sides, and he became an ally of the British. He contacted the enemy and decided to turn traitor.

General George Washington had put Arnold in charge of the key outpost on the Hudson River known as West Point. Arnold devised a plan to sell West Point to the British for twenty thousand pounds, thus significantly weakening the colonies and all but guaranteeing a British victory. Ultimately, Arnold's plans were discovered and foiled. Washington labeled him a traitor for his treasonous act, and he fled to Britain. Today many would argue that Benedict

Arnold committed the greatest act of treason in American history.

Yet it is not the greatest act of treason ever committed. That dubious distinction belongs to Adam and Eve.

Theirs was an act of cosmic treason that far exceeded the treachery of Benedict Arnold. It was the act of rebelling against God in the garden of Eden. What Adam and Eve did was indeed treason. They rebelled and committed cosmic treason against the sovereign, Creator God. They rebelled against His goodness. They rebelled against His grace. And ever since the garden of Eden, every human being has come into the world as a rebel. The Bible is clear. When Adam and Eve rebelled, we all rebelled (Rom. 5:12).

Yet the grand and gracious story line of the Bible is "God reaching down to be gracious to rebels." That's the whole story line of redemptive history. The Bible is the story of God's gracious pursuit of rebels. It's the story line of the Bible. It's the message of Jonah.

The prophecy of Jonah is God in gracious pursuit. In fact, the big story of the Bible is pictured for us in the four short chapters of Jonah. Chapter 1 is the narrative of *rebellion*. Chapter 2 is the narrative of *repentance*. Chapter 3 is the narrative of *redemption*. Chapter 4 is the narrative of *restoration*. God redeems repentant rebels and restores them to relationship with Him. This is the Bible. This is Jonah. It begins with rebellion.

A Rebellious Beginning

The prophecy of Jonah begins with these words:

> The word of the LORD came to Jonah son of Amittai: "Get up! Go to the great city of Nineveh and preach against it because their evil has come up before me." Jonah got up to flee to Tarshish from the LORD's presence. He went down to Joppa and found a ship going to Tarshish. He paid the fare and went down into it to go with them to Tarshish from the LORD's presence. (Jonah 1:1–3)

The prophecy of Jonah begins with rebellion. God sent Jonah to preach to a people in rebellion against God. Notice how it begins: "The word of the LORD came to Jonah" (v. 1). The word that came to Jonah was clear, and it was direct: "Get up! Go to the great city of Nineveh and preach against it because their evil has come up before me" (v. 2). God sent Jonah to a rebelling people. He sent him to Nineveh.

Nineveh was a great city by any measure of worldly standards. It was the capital city of the Assyrian Empire, which at the time was the most prominent and powerful empire on earth. It was a city that would have been known simply by its name, like New York, London, or Tokyo. It was the most prominent city in the most prominent nation in the land.

Moreover, Nineveh was filled with great things. It was filled with luscious and fabulous gardens. It was filled with a large and prosperous irrigation system. It was filled with great and impressive walls, huge displays of magnificent art, and grand libraries.

Business was booming in Nineveh—there was much commerce. It was also a paragon of education—there was much learning.

It was a large city. It was, as it says later in Jonah 3:3, "an extremely great city, a three-day walk" to traverse. It was populated by upward of 130,000 people at any time.

It was a city known by all, and like New York or London, you only had to say Nineveh, and everyone knew what city you were talking about. You knew where it was. You knew what it was.

Nineveh was a great city by any stretch of the imagination. But it was not only great for what it was; it was great also for what it did. It sinned. And it was full of evil.

Nineveh was Gotham. It was a great city given over to great sin. You can imagine that a large metropolis like this would be filled with the wickedness of human hearts, and indeed it was. It was filled with idolatry, greed, lust, murder, and all the wickedness of the human heart. It was filled with false worship. It was a pagan city and stood against the will and rule of God.

God sent Jonah to speak out against this pagan city. This was not Israel; this was Assyria. This was not Jerusalem or Bethlehem; this was Nineveh. These were not the people of God; these were the Ninevites.

This should remind us of an important principle—namely, all nations are accountable to God. All people and all nations are subject to God and must give an account of their lives. We know Israel was accountable before God, and oftentimes God called Israel to account. But do we know that God is Lord over all nations and not just Israel? The prophets of the Old Testament were not just sent to call Israel to get right with God, but at times the call was to the foreign nations as well. Amos prophesied of God's judgment against Damascus, Gaza, Edom, Tyre, Moab, and others (Amos 1–2). These nations were not recognized as God's chosen people. Yet God would call them to account before His throne of justice. He calls all nations. All people must give an account for their waywardness and their rebellion against God.

The psalmist says, "Why do the nations rage and the peoples plot in vain? . . . The one [God] enthroned in heaven laughs; the Lord ridicules them" (Ps. 2:1, 4). There is no people or nation on this earth who will not answer before God. Not a nation, not a people, and not a person who is not subject to God. Jesus is not simply the Lord of the church; Jesus is Lord of all (Rom. 14:7-8).

The church has long confessed this truth. Beginning in Philippians 2:5, we find one of the oldest confessions of the church. The confession ends with a glorious crescendo of the accountability of all creatures before the sovereign lordship of Jesus Christ. We are reminded that "every knee will bow— in heaven and on earth and under the earth—and every tongue will confess that Jesus Christ is Lord, to the glory of God the Father" (Phil. 2:10-11). Jesus is not simply Lord of the church; He is not simply Lord of the redeemed; He is Lord over all. Every knee shall bow, and every tongue shall confess. God reminded Jonah and the world that He is God over all. And He holds all accountable for their rebellion.

The remarkable thing is that God was gracious to these rebellious people. God sent His word to them through the mouth of His prophet. He showed grace to them by pursuing them. However, in this instance, the prophet was no different from the people. How's that for irony? God sent a rebelling prophet to rebelling people.

God told Jonah, "Get up! Go to . . . Nineveh" (Jonah 1:2). The word of the Lord was clear. The will of the Lord, in this instance, was clear. And yet Jonah's first instinct was to rebel because rebellion comes naturally.

We come into the world rebellious. You don't have to teach your children how to rebel; just leave them alone! Because we are by nature rebellious people, they instinctively know how to rebel. We rebel because we act as if we don't know what the will of God is. Yet, as it was to Jonah, the will of God is clearer than most of us want or are willing to admit.

Too many of us are searching around for the will of God as if it were some ever-illusive magical formula. And because we are unable discern what God's will is, we are content to live in disobedience. We spend our time chasing after and hoping for a word from God. Unfortunately, what we fail to do is look into *the* Word of God. Like Jonah, if you would look to the Word of God, you would find the will of God. God's will was clear because God's word was clear. It was that way to Jonah. It is that way to us. Do you want to know the will of God? It is clear if you go into the Word of God.

The will of God is clear. According to the Word of God, the will of God is for husbands to love their wives (Col. 3:19). The will of God is for wives to submit to their husbands (Col. 3:18). The will of God is for children to obey their parents (Col. 3:20). The will of God is that we abstain from sexual immorality (1 Thess. 4:3). It doesn't get any clearer than that. The will of God is that you and I would be growing in the grace and the knowledge of Jesus Christ (Col. 1:10). It is the will of God that you and I give thanks in all things (1 Thess. 5:18). As you can see, the will of God is clear if we would go to the Word of God to find it.

So it was with Jonah; there was no misunderstanding of what God wanted Jonah to do. He heard the Word of God. But rebellion is not rooted in ignorance. Rebellion is rooted in rank disobedience. Jonah didn't want to hear it. We don't want to know the will of God, and so we don't go to the Word of God. We want to rebel. And so instead of rising and going to Nineveh, Jonah rose and fled to Tarshish.

Tarshish was a place far away. You may wonder where it is. You may wonder about its geographical location or the coordinates of its global positioning. Yet the point is not so much where Tarshish is but what it represents.

Tarshish represents obstinacy and rebellion. It is the place children go to spite their parents. It is the place men and women go to hide from God. It is the place we convince ourselves we are out of sight and out of mind. Yet to think you are ever out of God's sight is to be out of your mind.

When God determines to save, there is no escape to Tarshish. No matter how far you try to go, you can't go far enough. No matter where you seek to hide, there is no hiding place (Ps. 139:7–8). In fact, Tarshish should remind us that no matter how hard you run, mercy runs harder. Mercy runs faster. Jonah thought Tarshish would save him from God. The wonderful truth is that God saved Jonah from Tarshish. He always does.

Perhaps many days have been spent wondering why God forbade a job, a move, a promotion, or even a relationship. Even though you ignored the warning signs and sought to silence God's voice, God didn't give in, nor did He give up on you. Instead, the mercy of God persisted until your eyes could see the truth. The grace of God relentlessly pursued you until the will of God was not only good for you but also good to you. Thankfully, you never made it to Tarshish.

I am sure there were people in Tarshish who needed to hear the Word of God, but that is not what God sent Jonah to do. How often do we do that? We rationalize our disobedience and our rebellion by thinking we can make something good come out of it. Jonah thought to himself, *I'll just go down to Tarshish, God. You send somebody else to Nineveh. I'll preach in Tarshish. I'm sure they need to hear the Word of God too.* Yet partial obedience is disobedience.

Partial obedience only leads to full disobedience. God told Jonah to rise. He rose, but that's where the obedience stopped. Instead of going east, Jonah went west. Instead of going north, Jonah went south. Instead of going to Nineveh, he went to Tarshish. Jonah was not just fleeing but also refusing to do the will of God.

Here's the real issue: Jonah was fleeing from the presence of God. It wasn't just that Jonah did not want to do what God had called him to do; Jonah didn't want anything to do with God Himself, and that's really the issue whenever we rebel. When we rebel against God's Word, we rebel against God. This was Jonah's problem. He was rebelling against God. Nevertheless, rebellious people and prophets don't stress God. God's not stressed by your rebellion, and you know why? Because God is resourceful.

Rebellious people and prophets do not stress God out because God has unlimited resources at His disposal, and what He doesn't yet have, He can create.

A Resourceful God

Jonah ran from God. And when he ran, Jonah discovered what everybody discovers when they run from God. When you run from God, you run smack into God.

In his sermon in *Moby Dick*, Father Mapple states, "He [Jonah] thinks that a ship made by men will carry him into countries where God does not reign." Father Mapple rightly captured the folly of humans running from God. Our God is a resourceful God, and we see the nature of His resourcefulness is grounded in His character. Who is this God that Jonah is rebelling against? Who is this God that we seek to run away from? The first thing you ought to know is that He is an *omnipresent* God.

Omnipresent

Omnipresence means that God is everywhere present. There is no place or space in the universe where God is not fully there.

Twice in verse 3 Jonah is said to have fled from the presence of the Lord. How does one escape the presence of the Lord? The impossibility is staggering if you just contemplate it for a moment. Where are you going? In Psalm 139:7–12, the psalmist says:

> Where can I go to escape your Spirit?
> Where can I flee from your presence?
> If I go up to heaven, you are there;
> if I make my bed in Sheol, you are there.
> If I live at the eastern horizon
> or settle at the western limits,
> even there your hand will lead me;
> your right hand will hold on to me.
> If I say, "Surely the darkness will hide me,

and the light around me will be night"—
even the darkness is not dark to you.
The night shines like the day;
darkness and light are alike to you.

Fleeing from God? Where are you going? In Jeremiah 23:23-24 God says:

"Am I a God who is only near . . . and not a
God who is far away? Can a person hide in
secret places where I cannot see him? . . . Do
I not fill the heavens and the earth?"

The idea of God's omnipresence is not that God is simply present or partially present; the idea is that He fills the place. He is fully present—in all of His being, character, and attributes—everywhere, at all times. Nothing and no one escapes His attention.

However, when you are in rebellion, the last person you want to see is God. The last person you want to hear is God. And so, like Jonah, you flee. You flee from the Word of God because you don't want to hear the will of God. But everywhere you go, there God is. You cannot get away from Him.

When we are rebelling, this seems like bad news. But it is actually great news. We should thank God that we cannot get away from Him.

Do you realize that the happiness in heaven and the horrors of hell are rooted in the same reality? The reality is the uncompromised holiness and justice of God. For the rebellious the justice of God is a horrible, terrible reality. For the redeemed it is their hope; it is their joy. Heaven is heaven because God is there in all of His goodness, giving those made righteous in Christ their reward. Hell is hell because there God's holiness is on display in the fullness of His wrath and righteous judgment. Everywhere you go it's the holiness and justice of God.

You cannot hide from God. A better course of action is to hide *in* God. You hide in Him, not from Him. "He hideth my soul," the songwriter says, "in the cleft of the rock."[1] Indeed, he does. It is God's delight for you to find refuge in Him. It is God's delight that you know Christ as that Rock in whom you can hide from the ravages of the wrath of God against rebellious sinners. You don't run from God; you run to Him. You don't hide from God, but rather by faith "your life is hidden with Christ in God" (Col. 3:3).

Omniscient

God is not only omnipresent; our God is *omniscient*. Omniscience is God being all-knowing. God not only knew where Jonah was, but God also knew where Jonah was going.

He not only knew that Jonah got up and was getting in the ship, but God knew where the ship was headed. God knew what Jonah was thinking. He not only saw him; He knew what was on his mind. He knew what was in his heart.

Omniscience is God's seeing all things. Omniscience is God's knowing all things. He knew the thoughts and intentions of Jonah's heart.

Jonah thought he was going to pull one over on God, yet the Bible says in Psalm 94:11, "The LORD knows the thoughts of mankind." He knows your thoughts. Psalm 139:2 says, "You understand my thoughts from far away." Genesis 6:5 reminds us that prior to sending the great flood, God knew "that every inclination of the human mind was nothing but evil all the time." God knows. Jeremiah 17:9-10 begins, "The heart is more deceitful than anything else, and incurable—who can understand it?" And then it goes on to say, "I, the LORD, examine the mind, I test the heart." God knows our hearts infinitely more than we can ever know them.

God knows you. No doubt, this is a terror for those seeking to flee from Him. He knows what you're planning before you plan it. He knows what you're devising and scheming before you set to devise and scheme it. He knows your intentions, and for those who are trying to flee from God, this is a terrible thought. But for those who are seeking to find comfort and refuge in God, this is a comfort. And this is why the psalmist could say with confidence in Psalm 139:23–24, "Search me, God, and know my heart; test me and know my concerns. See if there is any offensive way in me; lead me in the everlasting way." In other words, "I don't mind Your knowing me. I want You to know me. If You find anything of rebellion and wickedness in my heart, O Lord, reveal it, and I bid You to remove it in this hour."

That's the joy of knowing the Lord knows you. His knowledge of you calls you to repent of your sin, turn from your rebellion, and come to Him because you know there is no other refuge. And the amazing thing is, the Lord who delights to know you in spite of your rebellion is the one who loves you.

Have you ever contemplated, just for a moment, that He who knows you best loves you most? Now most people who love you, love you because they don't really know you. If they really knew you, would they love you? If they really knew your thoughts and the intents of your heart, if they knew all the things you are planning and scheming, would they love you still? Every human being longs to be fully known and fully loved, but we are all afraid that if we were fully known, we could never be fully loved. And yet He who knows you most loves you best.

This is just one of the many reasons I don't debate or long tolerate people who believe Christians, truly born again, can lose their salvation. He who saved me knew the worst about me when He saved me. While I was at my worst, Christ died for me (Rom. 5:8). Is some new information going to come to His attention that's going to suddenly make Him change His mind? Of course not! This is the comfort of the redeemed, "My God knows me, and I am still His." I want Him to know me. God's knowledge of me makes His love for me all the more precious because He knows me.

See how resourceful our God is? He's all-present. He's all-knowing. He's all-powerful also.

Omnipotent

God is *omnipotent*. Omnipotence is God being all-powerful. Jonah fled from God. Perhaps he thought God would find him too difficult to deal with. So he said, "Maybe I'll just be difficult," and God would say, "Ain't nobody got time to be dealing with Jonah. That nut is too hard to crack. Let Me go find someone who is a little more pliable. I ain't got time to be dealing with obstinate."

If the Bible makes one truth unmistakably clear, it is that the power of God is a beast. God's power is not subject to the whims of nature or the will of men.

Both Jonah and the sea were in the hands of El Shaddai, the all-powerful God. God is able to turn both the sea and Jonah any way He pleases. Jonah believed himself safe in the boat heading to Tarshish. However, in verse 4 we read, "The LORD threw a great wind onto the sea." God hurled a great wind. Why? Because God has a purpose. God has a plan. And His purposes and plans were not going to be thwarted by Jonah's schemes or obstinate rebellious ways.

Job 42:2 says, "I know that you can do anything and no plan of yours can be thwarted." If God had purposed for Jonah to go Nineveh, guess what was going to happen. You guessed it! Jonah was going to Nineveh.

Jonah underestimated the power of God and thought he could get in the ring with God. Like many of us, Jonah decided to fight with God. Even if we don't win, we think, *Perhaps we will resist long enough for God to get tired, frustrated, and to give in or give up.* Yet the truth is that the power of God never wanes, nor does He get exasperated. Instead, God hurled a great wind. God threw the wind upon the sea and then threw the sea against the ship.

The men onboard the ship began to fight for their lives. They were fighting against the wind. They were fighting against the sea. Yet they were not just fighting wind and wave. They were fighting against God. In a fight against the power and might of God, the best that men and women can do is to call upon their idols. And that's what the men onboard the ship did.

They cried out to their gods, "What shall we do? What are we going to do?" And the best their idols could tell them to do, apparently, was to lighten the load of the boat and throw some of the cargo overboard. Some bags overboard? That's the best their gods got? In essence, their gods said, "This great wind is being hurled against you. Hurl the bags. Hurl the suitcases." Their efforts were futile. Their gods' power and understanding amounted to nothing.

Concerning the power of the true and living God, Daniel 4:35 states:

> All the inhabitants of the earth are counted
> as nothing, and [God] does what he wants
> with the army of heaven and the inhabitants
> of the earth. There is no one who can block
> his hand or say to him, "What have you
> done?"

The sovereign power of God is a sweet and awful place. Think about it. Has God determined to save you? Do you know that nothing can stop Him? Nothing can thwart His plan. If His purpose is to redeem you, and to bring you into the knowledge of Jesus Christ, who can stop Him? He is prepared to expend any resource at His disposal. He is prepared to extend everything, including the life of His own Son. He is prepared to use all of His power to save you. As the singer says, "Ain't no mountain high enough. And ain't no valley low enough." And ain't no ship big enough to keep Him from getting to Jonah. Or to you. Or to me.

Unfortunately, like Jonah, when God calls most of us, we are sound asleep. It is usually a rebellious sleep.

A Rebellious Sleep

Rather than obey God, the Bible says, Jonah went to sleep. This is amazing. He went to sleep. When you are expected to be awake, few things are as offensive as being asleep. When you are in school and supposed to be paying attention, there are not too many more offensive things you can do than put your head on the desk and just go to sleep. When you are at work and supposed to be working, fulfilling the obligations and responsibilities for which you are paid, few things are as offensive as when the supervisor or the boss comes around and you are sound asleep. When you come to church, and the preacher is preaching, breathless and sweating, few things are as offensive as falling asleep. In fact, falling asleep when you should be awake can be life-threatening.

In the army, if you are on watch during wartime and you fall asleep, the penalty is a court-martial and possible execution, because few things are as offensive as falling asleep when you are supposed to be alert.

Perhaps this is why sleep is often spoken of in negative terms in the Bible. Proverbs 20:13 states, "Don't love sleep, or you will become poor" (see also Prov. 6:9–11). This is particularly true when we are commanded to stay awake. Jesus commanded His disciples, "But be alert at all times, praying that you may have strength to escape all these things that are going to take place and to stand before the Son of Man" (Luke 21:36).

Jonah was not just asleep. The Bible says that Jonah was in a deep sleep. While the wind was blowing and the waves were crashing, Jonah was fast asleep. He was literally sleeping in the midst of God's power. This rebellious sleep illustrates Jonah's spiritual numbness.

Jonah was in a deep sleep, and he was the only one sleeping. Indeed, there is a time to sleep but not in the midst of God's power. Not when God is working His wonder and revealing His will all around you. Not when God is calling you unto Himself and revealing His purpose for your life. Yet Jonah was spiritually numb. God was doing mighty things around Jonah, yet Jonah was sleeping. God was moving and showing Himself strong, yet Jonah was sleeping.

There is a time to sleep, but not on the gospel. Romans 1:16 states, "I am not ashamed of the gospel, because it is the power of God for salvation." Don't sleep in the midst of His power. Don't sleep when the power of God is at work all around you. Don't sleep as the gospel is being proclaimed. Wake up! Now is not the time to sleep. Don't you sleep on that 116! Stay woke!

Jonah slept in the midst of God's power. But he also slept in the midst of pagans. Who had to wake Jonah up? It was the unbelievers. Jonah may have slept on what God was doing, but the unbelievers weren't sleeping. They knew something was going on. They knew something was wrong. They knew a power was inherent in this storm that they had never experienced before. They knew that now was not the time to sleep. They didn't know all that was going on, but they knew something was not right.

There is a unique shame upon our spiritual numbness when the watching world can look at Christians in the church and know something is wrong, yet we seem to be asleep to it. In 1 Corinthians 5:1, Paul indicted the church in Corinth for tolerating obvious sexual immorality. Paul said, "It is actually reported that there is sexual immorality among you, and the kind of sexual immorality that is not even tolerated among the Gentiles" It is shameful that the hearts of God's people could be so numb to the will and the way of God that even unbelievers know something is wrong, and the church is blind to it. It is the sign of falling asleep in the midst of God's power and in the midst of pagans.

If any people should know the need for justice in this world, it is Christians. Those in the world know that something is wrong when police abuse their authority and misuse their weapons. Those in the world know that something is wrong when our incarceration rates continue to increase while our graduation rates decrease. When God is shaking the foundations of our society, even the watching world knows something is wrong. Yet too many Christians are like Jonah—sound asleep.

No one knows justice like Christians do. No one should decry inhumane treatments and the abuse of power like Christians should. God has told us what is good and what He requires—for us to act justly, love mercy, and walk humbly before our God (Mic. 6:8). Let us stay woke!

And yet here is the patience of the grace of God: God is not averse to using the unrepentant to awaken the repentant so that the repentant may demonstrate repentance to the unrepentant.

In other words, God will use the ungodly to wake up the godly so the godly will repent and show the ungodly what repentance looks like. And so God did with Jonah. God used these pagan men. They came and awoke Jonah. They said, "Wake up, O Sleeper! Wake up!"

Here is the irony of ironies. They say to Jonah what Jonah should have been saying to Nineveh. "Get up! Call to your God. Maybe this god will consider us, and we won't perish" (Jonah 1:6). There it is—grace to the rebels. God was not going to let Jonah stay asleep. He came in power to wake Jonah up. He does the same thing for you and me.

God is not going to let you stay asleep. He's coming. He is going to use all of His power to finally wake you up because His desire is to pursue rebels unto bringing them into the knowledge and the will of God. What a marvelous, grace-filled word and thought this is: *Maybe this god will consider us, and we won't perish.* Perhaps, if you get up and call on God, He will be gracious. Get up and call on God. Perhaps He will be merciful. And the operative word here is *perhaps*.

Perhaps is the operative word because salvation isn't owed to anyone. Perhaps, God will be gracious because salvation is always by grace. God is not obligated at all to deal with any of us contrary to what we actually deserve. Jonah was a rebel. Jonah was treasonous. And like Nineveh, Jonah deserved death. "But Jonah, if you would get up and call on God, perhaps He would be gracious. Perhaps He will see your need, and perhaps He will grant you mercy."

You know rebels don't deserve mercy. Traitors deserve to be hung. They deserve to be executed. And if you are anything like me, then you know that your life is that of a rebel.

You know where you have come from. You know where you were when you were in rebellion against God. You know how rebellion marked out every thought and intent of your heart. The only hope rebels have is the mercy of God. The message of Jonah is, "Stop the rebellion!" Stop the rebellion and cry out to God for mercy.

I am confident that if you call on God for mercy today, God *will* (not just *perhaps*) be merciful to you. He will be merciful because now is the time and today is the day of salvation. He sent to you one greater than Jonah, and His name is Jesus; and He says, "Wake up! Salvation has come to your home and your heart today. Wake up!" Stop rebelling. His will is best. Stop running. Stop hiding. Find your rest in Him.

A. W. Tozer was right when he said that Jesus came to earth "to make worshippers out of rebels."[2] That's why you say, "Hallelujah!" Because grace and hope have come to the rebellious. Awake and sing hallelujah! Christ redeems, owns, and loves rebels!

You Can't Outrun God

Jonah 1:7–16

———

"Come on!" the sailors said to each other. "Let's cast lots. Then we'll know who is to blame for this trouble we're in." So they cast lots, and the lot singled out Jonah. Then they said to him, "Tell us who is to blame for this trouble we're in. What is your business, and where are you from? What is your country, and what people are you from?"

He answered them, "I'm a Hebrew. I worship the LORD, the God of the heavens, who made the sea and the dry land."

Then the men were seized by a great fear and said to him, "What is this you've done?" The men knew he was fleeing from the LORD's presence because he had told them. So they said to him, "What should we do to you so that the sea will calm down for us?" For the sea was getting worse and worse.

He answered them, "Pick me up and throw me into the sea so that it will calm down for you, for I know that I'm to blame for this great storm that is against you." Nevertheless, the men rowed hard to get back to dry land, but they couldn't because the sea was raging against them more and more.

So they called out to the LORD: "Please, LORD, don't let us perish because of this man's life, and don't charge us with innocent blood! For you, LORD, have done just as you pleased." Then they picked up Jonah and threw him into the sea, and the sea stopped its raging. The men were seized by great fear of the LORD, and they offered a sacrifice to the LORD and made vows.

Francis Thompson was born in the mid-nineteenth century in England to a well-to-do Roman Catholic family. His father was a physician, and his parents wanted him to be a physician as well. However, he detested the occupation and wanted to be a writer. His family insisted, so he went to medical school.

Following medical school, he failed the medical exam three times. After failing the exam the last time, he ran from his home and fled to London, where he hoped to become a writer. Unfortunately for him, things didn't pan out exactly as he had hoped. He ended up getting a few odd jobs trying to make ends meet and before long found himself out on the streets. It wasn't long before he was addicted to opium.

His father often sent him money. Since Thompson didn't have a permanent address, his father would send the money in the care of a local library. Yet frequently the library wouldn't let Thompson in because he looked so shabby.

One day a prostitute found him on the street nearly dead. Once he was nursed back to relative health, he began to write. When it became known that he was a writer, a local family befriended him and began to publish some of his writings in the local papers. People began to see that there was a great writer among them, but no one knew exactly who it was. Francis Thompson eventually died due to complications from addiction and indigent living. His most famous poem tells his story. It's called "The Hound of Heaven," and it reads:

> I fled Him, down the nights and down the
>   days;
> I fled Him, down the arches of the years;
> I fled Him, down the labyrinthine in ways
> of my own mind; and in the midst of tears
> I hid from Him, and under running
>   laughter.[3]

Thompson thought himself running from God. He fled from God in the country. He fled from God in the streets of London. He fled from God in addiction and dereliction. And yet to Thompson's exhaustion, he believed God hounded him and hounded him. Keenly aware of this pursuit, Thompson wrote "The Hound of Heaven," stating, "I fled Him, but everywhere I fled Him, He hounded me."

Jonah is the biblical account of "The Hound of Heaven." No doubt Jonah knew he was running with God in pursuit. But what Jonah soon learned (and I pray that you and I would learn it too), was that he couldn't outrun God. You can't outrun God's truth. You can't outrun God's justice. You can't outrun God. From Jonah 1:7-16, thankfully, we learn the truth that *you can't outrun the providence of God, you can't outrun your sin, and you can't outrun God's grace.*

You Can't Outrun the Providence of God

What is providence? Providence is simply the idea of God ordaining and maintaining the universe according to His will. It is God governing and working all things out for His glory and the praise of His name. It is God providing, caring, orchestrating, and guiding the cares, events, and people of this world. The Heidelberg Catechism describes providence as:

> The Almighty, ever-present power of God, by
> which He upholds as with His hand heaven
> and earth, and all creatures, and so rules
> them that leaf and blade, rain and drought,
> fruitful and lean years, food and drink,
> health and sickness, prosperity and poverty,
> all things, in fact, come to us not by chance
> but from His fatherly hand.[4]

Wilhelmus à Brakel, a seventeenth-century theologian, wrote that "the providence of God pertains to everything, is so clearly revealed in nature and in Scripture that whoever denies the providence of God is no better than an atheist or, at best, must be as blind as a mole."[5]

God ordains and executes His will throughout all creation. When Jonah refused to heed the call of God to Nineveh and instead tried to go down to Tarshish, he discovered two things about the providence of God: Jonah discovered that God is providentially in control of the elements and that God is in control of events.

God Is in Control of the Elements

Jonah thought he could escape from the hand and the will of God, but he discovered that he had as much chance of escaping God as he had of outrunning the wind. While the rest of the men on the boat were seeking to understand the source of the tempest, Jonah knew. He knew it was the only true God, who controls and sustains even the elements of nature. In Amos 4:7 God says, "I sent rain on one city but no rain on another." God is in control of the elements. All human beings know this. In fact, we seem to know it instinctively.

Whether one has faith in Jesus Christ or not, when the elements rage, we refer to them as "acts of God." This is done among the religious and the irreligious alike. From newspapers to newscasters, from tornadoes to tsunamis, that which is beyond human control is referred to as an "act of God." Yet "act of God" is not foreign to the Scriptures. In fact, Psalm 147:15 plainly states:

> He sends his command throughout the
> earth;
> his word runs swiftly.
> He spreads snow like wool;
> he scatters frost like ashes;
> he throws his hailstones like crumbs.
> Who can withstand his cold?
> He sends his word and melts them;
> he unleashes his winds, and the water flows.

Whatever the forecast, the Bible affirms it is an "act of God." This should be a comfort in your life. It is comforting to know that God is in control of all the elements not only when the storms hit the world but also when the storms come crashing upon our lives.

Recall Mark 4, when Jesus was in the boat on the Sea of Galilee with His disciples, and He was asleep. A storm like the disciples had never seen before began to rage, and the disciples feared for their lives. They woke Jesus and said, "Teacher! Don't you care that we're going to die?" (v. 38). Jesus looked at them as if to say, "Of course I care. In fact, I care more than you do. O you of little faith." Then He looked at the wind, and He looked at the waves, and He spoke the words, "Silence! Be still." The Bible says, "The wind ceased, and there was a great calm" (v. 39). The disciples looked at one another and asked, "Who then is this? Even the wind and the sea obey him!" (v. 41).

Jesus spoke to the waves just as He speaks to his sheep (John 10:27). They know His voice. They hear Him, and they obey. Nature and the natural elements are no different to Jesus than sheep are to a shepherd. The waves and the wind knew their Lord's voice, and when they heard it, they obeyed.

Again, this is a great comfort to us because there are no storms that are not subject to our Lord's will. Whether in nature, in your home, or in your heart, there are no storms that are not subject to the will of our Lord. In fact, it would be a great concern and distress to learn that there is a storm or trial in your life over which God had no control.

You want God in control. You need God in control. Our prayers are essentially, "O God, please be in control." It is comforting to know that there is not a test or trial or affliction that comes to me that did not come from God. Because then I know He can and He will work it out for my good. Because then I know when I call on Him, He can actually do something about it. Because He is in control. Consequently, that's why we can sing:

I sing the mighty power of God that made the
　　mountains rise,
that spread the flowing seas abroad and built the
　　lofty skies.
I sing the wisdom that ordained the sun to rule
　　the day;
the moon shines full at his command, and all the
　　stars obey.[6]

Nothing of the elements is outside of God's sovereign will.

Interestingly, you may have noticed an allusion in the story of Jesus asleep on the boat to the story of Jonah asleep on the boat. Funny how God works like that. Jonah was sleeping when he wasn't supposed to be, and it was greatly offensive to the other men on the boat. They were in the midst of a storm caused by God, that only God could stop. And what needed to be done for God to stop the storm? Jonah needed to be tossed overboard.

Likewise, Jesus was sleeping when, apparently, He wasn't supposed to be, and it was greatly offensive to the other men on the boat. They, too, were in the midst of a storm caused by God, that only God could stop. And what needed to be done for God to stop the storm? Jesus, God the Son, only needed to speak the word.

We want Jesus in our boat. Whether our seas are currently placid and peaceful or raging and seemingly out of control, we want Jesus in our boat. Even when He seems to be asleep, He is with us and He is for us. Unlike Jonah, the solution isn't to kick Jesus out of the boat; the solution is to turn to Him and trust that He has power over the storms in our lives. In His providence God is working the elements together for our good.

Not only is He in control of the elements, but He is also in control of the events.

God Is in Control of Events

When the men on the boat with Jonah sought to know the reason for their sudden misfortune, the Bible says, "So they cast lots, and the lot singled out Jonah" (Jonah 1:7). What were lots? In biblical times lots were used in various ways to discern the divine will. Believers and unbelievers used it. It was a common practice. In fact, on occasion, God even ordained the use of lots. In Leviticus 16:8, for example, the lot is used for selecting animals for the offering. In Numbers 26:55–56 and in Joshua 14:2, we see that the lots were used for dividing the land among the tribes of Israel. In 1 Samuel 10:20–21 Saul was chosen king by lot.

In the New Testament, when the disciples had gathered together on the day of Pentecost, they decided that someone must replace Judas in order to make the number of the apostles twelve again. How did they choose the disciple who would replace Judas? They cast lots, and the lot fell on Matthias (Acts 1:26). But what were lots?

We don't know exactly what they were. They were something akin to perhaps rolling dice or drawing straws or playing rock, paper, scissors. Whatever they were, those who used them were looking for the will of God through what seems to have been a random, fortuitous, chance-taking event.

Yet they were not just drawing straws. They were not just playing rock, paper, scissors. According to the Bible there is no such thing as random and chance events. God is like Jason Bourne; he doesn't do random. God's people don't do lucky. Amazingly, there are no random events, not even in the casting of lots. Proverbs 16:33 says, "The lot is cast into the lap, but its every decision is from the LORD." God is in control of all events.

Kingdoms come, and kingdoms go. Kings rise, and kings fall. Presidents and mayors get elected, and presidents and mayors leave office, all according to the sovereign plan and providential will of God. Daniel 2:20–21 reminds us:

> May the name of God
> be praised forever and ever,
> for wisdom and power belong to him.
> He changes the times and seasons;
> he removes kings and establishes kings.
> He gives wisdom to the wise
> and knowledge to those
> who have understanding.

Knowledge to those who have understanding comes from God. Consequently, the knowledge of Jonah's being the cause of the storm did not come from the casting of lots. Ultimately, it came from God. Let us not put too much stock in casting lots; knowledge didn't come from the lots but from God.

Knowledge, wisdom, and insight come from God. It is important that you and I see the hand of God in all the affairs of our lives. Always see God at work in your life. Like Joseph from the pit to the prison to the palace, God had his hand on Joseph the whole way. God has his hand on you too. Do you see it? Are you observing it?

The Puritans would say, "He who observes providence has providence to observe." In other words, if you are careful to look around and look for the hand of God in your life, you will see the hand of God in your life. And consequently, the more you see, the more you will see. You will see that all creation, great and small, belongs to Him.

Don't think for a moment that the song "He's Got the Whole World in His Hands" is just a ditty for kiddies. It is full of some of the simplest and yet most profound theology you could ever sing. Our God does have the whole world in His hands.

Be quick to see the hand of God in the events and the affairs of your life because even though the sailors had yet to see it, you know who did observe that providence? Jonah. Jonah could see the invisible hand of God tracking him all the way. It brought him face-to-face with his sin.

You Can't Outrun Your Sin

Jonah observed the invisible hand of God in the events surrounding him. He knew it was God because he came to understand that he could not outrun his sin. In seeking to outrun God, Jonah was trying to outsprint his sin. He was trying to outdistance his disobedience. Numbers 32:23 clearly tells us, "Be sure your sin will catch up with you." When you seek to run from your sin, there will eventually be a confrontation.

You're Eventually Going to Be Confronted

Once the lot fell on Jonah, the sailors went to him and asked, "Tell us who is to blame for this trouble we're in" (1:8). They confronted him because his sin no longer affected just him.

That's one reason eventually there is going to be a confrontation. You and I need to understand that our sin rarely, if ever, affects only us.

The sailors knew something was amiss. This was a storm unlike any they had ever known. And now Jonah's sin was putting them in peril. This is a principle the Bible illustrates over and over again.

In Joshua 7, Achan sinned by doing contrary to what God commanded the nation Israel to do. Achan's disobedience caused difficulty and hardship for the whole nation. When David, in 2 Samuel 24, took a census and counted the people against the will of God, seventy thousand people died on his account. Yet, arguably, the worst of them all was the sin of Adam.

When Adam and Eve sinned in the garden of Eden, it didn't just affect Adam and Eve. Romans 5:12 reminds us: "Therefore, just as sin entered the world through one man [Adam], and death through sin, in this way death spread to all people, because all sinned." Adam's sin enslaved all humanity to sin and death.

You should always remember that your sin never affects only you. This is the reason you can't outrun your sin: because it will affect those around you. Sons and daughters, your sin affects your parents. Husbands, your sin affects your wives. Wives, your sin affects your husbands. Fathers and mothers, your sin affects your children. Christians, your sin affects your fellow church members, your family, your friends, and your community. Your sin affects others. And therefore, God will bring it to light. God says, "For my gaze takes in all their ways. They are not concealed from me, and their iniquity is not hidden from my sight" (Jer. 16:17).

God knows. And He not only knows, but He reveals. "[God] reveals deep and hidden things; he knows what is in the darkness, and light dwells with him" (Dan. 2:22). God is going to reveal it. And when God confronts and reveals our sin, the true child of God will acknowledge it for what it is. And that's what Jonah did.

You're Going to Have to Acknowledge Your Sin

Following the confrontation Jonah acknowledged, "I can't run anymore. I know what's going on." Jonah was not ignorant of his disobedience. We rarely are. When Jonah was confronted with his disobedience, he acknowledged that his sin had caused their peril. Jonah didn't make excuses.

Unfortunately, excuses and justifications are too frequently our first retorts. When we are confronted with our sin, the first thing we frequently do is make excuses.

"I know I shouldn't have said that, but . . ."

"I know he's not saved and we shouldn't be together, but . . ."

"I know I shouldn't be doing this, but . . ."

In our disobedience we offer too many *buts*. Jonah made none. In fact, he admitted who he was and said, "I am a Hebrew. I know what's going on. I'm a Hebrew. I'm not ignorant of these things." He knew he was different. He knew God had called him out. He knew he was set apart for God's service. Today he would say, "I am a Christian. I know I should be doing better than that. I know that I should not be living in this disobedience. I understand God's will. No excuses. I am a child of God. I am called by His Spirit. I know I am a Christian." Unfortunately, too often we say, "I know I'm a Christian, and I know I shouldn't be doing that, *but* . . ."

Jonah didn't give a *but*. Instead, he admitted and acknowledged who he was. And even more, he acknowledged that he knew God, saying plainly, "I'm a Hebrew. I worship the LORD, the God of the heavens, who made the sea and the dry land" (1:9). He admitted to the sailors: "I am not ignorant of what's going on here. I know why the waves are crashing against the boat. I know why the wind is blowing. I know why the storm is raging. I am not ignorant of who God is. He is Yahweh. He is the sovereign, living God."

The sailors in response were incredulous. They said to him, "What is this that you have done! What in the world have you done to get us into this predicament. Why are you fleeing from the presence of God?"

We can look at Jonah and be reminded again that our sin will find us out. God loves us too much to allow us just to stay in sin. Listen, if you go on sinning, and the Lord doesn't bring conviction and confrontation, you need to reconsider your relationship with God. If you go on sinning, and there is nothing in your heart that is pulling you away from it, you should fear for your soul. I pray that God will prick my heart every day because it reminds me that I belong to Him. I pray that He will point out my sin every day because it says that He cares and He wants me on the right path; He wants me in the way of His obedience. He wants me in faith.

Many people are offended when God points out their sin. *God is a God of love,* they think, *so He will just overlook my sin.* But the reality is, the reason God doesn't just overlook our sin is because He loves us; He loves us too much to leave us in sin. He wants more for us.

Don't get too offended when your sin is pointed out. In fact, don't get offended by the pointer, be offended by the sin, and thank God that He loved you enough to care, to point out your disobedience. Be grateful for His goodness in pointing out your sin and thus pointing you to His grace.

You Can't Outrun God's Grace

The reason God won't let you stay in sin is that He delights for you to delight in His grace. The reason you can't outrun your sin is that God is determined to catch you and show you that you can't outrun His grace. That's what happened to Jonah.

It is inexplicable that sinners rebel against a good God. And yet we do it all the time. When we think about the goodness of God and all He has done for us, instead of crying out, "Hallelujah!", we rebel and live in disobedience. In our moments of clarity, we know this is inexplicable. Still, even more inexplicable is that this good God pursues and delights to redeem those who rebel against Him. Just think about that. He's good to you, you rebel and run from Him, and then He comes and pursues you so He can be good to you again. Honestly, that is beyond our comprehension because few, if any, would do that.

Suppose I was overly good to you. I fed you and clothed you. Suppose I lovingly took care of you, provided for you, and went out of my way to do all those things that you needed. And suppose in response you turned around and spat in my face and ran out the door. Would I come after you?

I would think myself good if I even left the door open in case you ever got the mind to come back home. I would think myself gracious if I even left a place at the table for you. In fact, I could line up a hundred Christians who would say, "You're doing good." A lot of them would even say, "You're doing more than I would!"

But God doesn't just leave the door open. God doesn't just put a plate at the table. He comes chasing after you. And He is not going to stop until He gets you. Goodness and mercy shall pursue you all the days of your life (Ps. 23:6). This is what happened with Jonah—goodness and mercy came running!

You might think that once the lot identified Jonah and the reason for the storm was revealed and Jonah admitted his disobedience, things would begin to calm down. Perhaps things would get back to normal. But that was not what Jonah told them. Instead, Jonah said, "Pick me up and throw me into the sea so that it will calm down for you, for I know that I'm to blame for this great storm that is against you" (1:12). Jonah knew admission of guilt was not enough.

Did you know the goal of God is not just the admission of our sin? The ultimate desire of God is that we would also acknowledge our need of Him and rejoice in His grace to us. God's ultimate goal is that we worship Him. In fact, that's the end for which we preach. The end of preaching is the glory of God and the joy of His people in the magnification of His love and grace. It is the glory of rejoicing in the grace and the goodness of God in redeeming us from our sin. That's God's design. That's His desire. That's His end. That's why the storm didn't stop.

Jonah told the sailors, "Throw me overboard. The storm will stop." But the sailors didn't listen to Jonah. Why would they? He's the reason they were in the mess. Plus, after they found out His God was powerful enough to bring this storm, they didn't want to get on God's bad side by throwing this Hebrew overboard. So, rather than listening to Jonah, the sailors decided they were going to spare his life. They headed for the shore. They started rowing. They rowed and they rowed. Yet the more they rowed, the more the sea raged.

Here is the surprising, unstoppable grace of God: God brought them to the end of themselves. The more they rowed, the worse it became. And once they realized their efforts only made things worse, they stopped rowing.

The blessed truth is that you won't know the grace of God until you give up trying to save yourself. When you come to the realization that you can't get yourself to the shore. When you realize you can't get yourself out of the storm of sin in your life. When you realize you need to put the oar down. Then you are going to experience the grace of God.

Ephesians 2:8 reminds us that "you are saved by grace through faith, and this is not from yourselves." You don't save yourself. You can't. When you come to the end of yourself you experience the salvation of the Lord. The sailors came to the end of themselves. And when they came to the end of themselves, they cried: "Please, LORD, don't let us perish because of this man's life, and don't charge us with innocent blood! For you, LORD, have done just as you pleased" (Jonah 1:14). These sailors recognized that Yahweh is God. They recognized that Yahweh does as He pleases (Ps. 115:3). And they recognized that only Yahweh could save them. Consequently, they did the only thing they could do: they called upon the name of the Lord, who promises to save everyone who calls upon His name (Joel 2:32; Acts 2:21; Rom. 10:13).

Here is the glory of it all. When you come to an end of yourself, you will find God. That's where God is. He is at the end of you. And that's where the sailors found Him. This is where God always is. This was where Jonah introduced them to God.

Jonah was supposed to be going to Nineveh to preach God—to preach salvation through God. The irony is that Jonah was on that boat because he refused to preach to unbelievers, and in the midst of the storm Jonah began to preach to unbelievers. Jonah began to do what God had ordained Jonah to do—namely, to proclaim the name of the Lord (even if he didn't do it with the right attitude or posture). And for the first time we see Jonah speak the name of his God.

He said, "I'm a Hebrew. I worship the LORD, the God of the heavens" (Jonah 1:9). The Lord, Yahweh, the God of heaven—this is the name God gave to His people, the name by which they were to know Him. This is the name of the God of Abraham, and Isaac, and Jacob. This is the holy name of God, the God who revealed Himself to Moses and said, "I am that I am" (Exod. 3:14 KJV). It's that name. In fact, when Moses asked God, "Who are you? Tell me who you are." God said in Exodus 34:6–7:

> The LORD—the LORD [Yahweh] is a compassionate and gracious God, slow to anger and abounding in faithful love and truth,

maintaining faithful love to a thousand generations, forgiving iniquity, rebellion, and sin. But he will not leave the guilty unpunished.

That's who He is. He is Yahweh. That's the covenant, faithful name of God. That is the name God has given to His people whereby they would know Him, enter into covenant with Him, have their sins forgiven, and receive the everlasting love and mercy of God. The Lord, Yahweh!

When the pagan sailors stopped rowing and came to the end of themselves, what did they do? They prayed. This time, however, they didn't pray to some distant, abstract god; they prayed to the living Lord. They call upon Yahweh, "O Lord." They prayed and pleaded: "O Lord, have mercy and let us not perish" (Jonah 1:14). They prayed to the God of heaven and earth. They prayed to the covenant, faithful God. They prayed to the only God who ordained their dire circumstances and could do anything about their circumstances.

They pleaded with God, "Please, LORD, don't let us perish because of this man's life, and don't charge us with innocent blood!" Yet they not only prayed to God and pleaded with God, but they also offered praised to God. They said, "For you, LORD, have done just as you pleased" (1:14).

At first glance one might think these men took the name of the Lord in vain. Were they sincere, or were they simply exhausting all "god" options? Actually, it seems they were taking the name of God upon their lips because they had come to understand that there was no rescue for them outside of God. There was no salvation for them outside of the covenant God of Abraham, Isaac, Jacob, and Jonah.

This should serve as a reminder to us. It is not enough just to know a god; you have to know the true God. It is not enough just to know about God. You have to know His name. And what is that name? The Bible tells us His name is salvation. The Bible tells us His name is wonderful. The Bible tells us the Lord God of heaven and earth has revealed His name to us intimately. He came to earth and took on the name above all names. His name is Jesus (Matt. 1:21). He is the Lord. There is no other name today through which salvation comes (Acts 4:12). You must know His name.

Don't simply call on God. The revelation of God has progressed, and it has become fuller than Jonah knew. Today when you call on God, you must call on Jesus. It is not simply calling on God. You can call on God until the cows come home. If you don't know His name is Jesus, and that the only way to the Father is through the Son, there is no hope; there is no salvation. His name means salvation. His name is power. His name is hope. His name is Jesus.

And "there is no other name under heaven given to people by which we must be saved" (Acts 4:12). What is the name? The name is Jesus!

That's His name! That's the self-revealed name of the covenant, faithful God, who comes to save when you come to the end of yourself. His name is Jesus. There is no sweeter name. In the call of those men on that boat to Yahweh, I hear myself calling on Jesus.

I know in my life that there has been no sweeter name than the name of Jesus. Oh, that all would call on Him. Call on Him with all of your being. Call on Him with everything you have. Call on Jesus and pray that God would be so gracious and reveal Himself to you and allow you to know the name. Call on Him, for there is salvation in no other. Oh, how sweet the name of Jesus! There is no sweeter name. In Him is salvation. In Him is grace. In Him is eternal life. Call on Jesus and be saved today.

3

Divine Appointments
Jonah 1:17–2:2

———

The LORD *appointed a great fish to swallow Jonah, and Jonah*
was in the belly of the fish three days and three nights.
Jonah prayed to the LORD *his God from the belly of the fish:*

I called to the LORD, *in my distress,*
and he answered me.
I cried out for help from deep inside Sheol;
you heard my voice.

Those who know me know I don't like being late. As my wife can testify, I can be fastidious about it. I don't like to break appointments. I don't like to cancel meetings. However, as we all know, sometimes circumstances deem that meetings have to be cancelled and appointments have to be postponed. Sometimes, unfortunately, people have to be late. And even though I don't like to break appointments, I will admit that there are some appointments I wish I could break.

At least once a year, my dentist's office calls me and says, "Mr. Carter, we haven't seen you in almost a year. It's about time that you came in to see the dentist for a checkup." I make the appointment, but as the day draws near, I look for every reason under the sun to cancel that early morning appointment.

Appointments with God

Here is a status update for you: *You don't break appointments with God.* There are some appointments we may desire to break, and there are some appointments we may need to break, but you don't break appointments made by God. Apparently, like many of us, Jonah forgot to read that memo. He deleted that email before he read it. But if he had read it, he would have seen, "Jonah, God has an appointment with you." God keeps His appointments and has every intention of making sure we do too.

When the word of God came to Jonah, it was clear: "Jonah you have an appointment with God in Nineveh. Get there on time." God wanted to meet Jonah in Nineveh so that God could work redemption and salvation among the Ninevites. Jonah, apparently, had other plans.

Rather than meet God in Nineveh, Jonah decided he was going to seek to cancel the appointment. But God's appointments are not invitations. God didn't invite Jonah to meet him in Nineveh. He commanded him. He had already planned it, and no one thwarts God's plans.

By resisting God, Jonah had to learn the hard way that God keeps His appointments. When God wants to get something done in us, and through us, or by us, He has the appointed means, He ordains the appointed times, and He consequently brings it to His appointed ends.

Appointed Means

God has the appointed means. One of the most remarkable sentences in the entire Scriptures is found in Jonah 1:17: "The LORD appointed a great fish to swallow up Jonah." What a remarkable word and an amazing revelation. It is a magnificent demonstration of the power and majesty of

God. "The LORD appointed a great fish to swallow Jonah." Every time I think about that, I stand amazed. It's remarkable. It is a testimony to the grandeur of God's ability and working in this world and in our lives. It is a monument to His majesty. "The LORD appointed a great fish to swallow Jonah." It reminds us that God has an endless supply of resources at His disposal. And when He decides it is necessary to use these appointed means, we are often left speechless because God's appointed means are inexplicable.

The appointment of this great fish to swallow Jonah reminds us that not only was the fish great, but more important, we worship a great God. *He who appoints is greater than that which is appointed.* It reminds us that a great God has great means often beyond our explanation.

For example, how do you explain this great fish swallowing Jonah? Many have tried, and all have come up short. I am convinced that Jonah would have tried but would have been at a loss for words. Imagine Jonah trying to explain his ordeal once he got back on shore.

Imagine he ran across the captain of the boat and the sailors who were with him. No doubt they were convinced Jonah had gone to his watery grave. They see Jonah walking again and incredulously ask, "Jonah, how did you get here? How did you survive the sea? How did you manage to live?"

And Jonah says, "Well, you wouldn't believe me if I told you."

"Try me."

"Really, you're not going to believe it."

"No? Try me!"

"Well, when you guys threw me overboard, I was sinking into the depths of the ocean. Suddenly, this huge fish came along and swallowed me. And I was in the belly of this fish for three days and three nights. And then the next thing I knew the fish decided he no longer wanted me in the bowels of his body, and he vomited me back up on shore. And here I am talking to you."

"You're right, Jonah. I don't believe you."

The truth is that when God decides to move and accomplish His will in the world, He often uses inexplicable means. How do you explain it? How do you explain in Exodus 3:2 a bush that burns but doesn't burn up? How do you explain in Numbers 22:28-30 a prophet riding a donkey and suddenly that donkey turns around and begins to prophesy to him? How do you explain it? How do you explain that eternal life comes to us through the foolishness of human preaching? These things are inexplicable. You don't fully explain them; you never can. The apostle Paul exults in Romans 11:33, "Oh, the depth of the riches both of the wisdom and of the knowledge of God! How unsearchable his judgments and untraceable his ways!"

The songwriter William Cowper summed it up well: "God moves in mysterious ways his wonders to perform; He sets his footsteps in the sea, and he rides upon the storm."[7] Because his ways are inexplicable, we are left to exclaim, "O for a thousand tongues"[8] to explain the ways of God in my world and in my life.

If you have a relationship with God that is easily and always explainable, you don't have a relationship with the Almighty King of heaven. Your faith must have a mystery. There must be inexplicable ways in which God has been working and moving in your life that as you give testimony to them, eventually you say, "I can't explain it. But I know what He has done. And my standing on this shore is evidence that God has done this." Or as the blind man said in John 9:25, after being inexplicably healed by Jesus, "One thing I do know: I was blind, and now I can see!"

God's means are not only inexplicable, but they are also unforgettable. This fish, this great fish, have you ever forgotten it since the first time you heard it? All you have to do is tell the story of Jonah to a child one time and they will never forget it. You don't forget that God appointed a great fish to swallow Jonah because His appointed means are not only inexplicable, but His appointed means are unforgettable.

When God does it, you don't forget it. This is God's way of doing things.

Some moments and movements of God in history are simply unforgettable. You and I don't have to be reminded of them because they are practically imprinted on our hearts and minds. I don't have to remind you how many commandments there are—you know there are ten. I don't have to remind you how many plagues there were in Egypt—you know there were ten. I don't have to remind you that Noah built the ark; you just don't forget that type of thing. I don't have to remind you that David slew Goliath; his victory is unforgettable. And I don't have to remind you that Jonah was swallowed by a great fish because you just don't forget these wonderful, mighty, powerful acts of God.

When God delights to move in your life to rescue you, to redeem you, to save you, you have no doubt who did it. In fact, recently I was speaking to a young man, and he was sharing with me his testimony. I was encouraged by how easily he recalled what God had done. He said, "The only explanation I have for no longer being trapped in sin is that God took that sin away from me, and I haven't forgotten it."

When God moves mightily in your life, to change your life, to change your heart from a heart of stone to a heart of flesh; when He opens your blinded eyes; when He transforms your wicked mind into a mind that seeks after Him and His righteousness, you don't forget it. The psalmist says, "My soul, bless the LORD, and do not forget all his benefits" (Ps. 103:2). How can you?

Can you imagine the psalmist getting up every morning and looking in the mirror? What does he see? He looks in the mirror and remembers the grace of God and the mercy of God upon a rebellious sinner. He looks at his children and is reminded of just how good and gracious God has been to him. He looks at his wife and is reminded of how undeserving he is. He cannot forget the benefits and blessings of God. Someone has rightly sung,

I never shall forget what the Lord has done for me.[9]

Appointed Times

Appointed means come at appointed times. "The LORD appointed a great fish to swallow Jonah, and Jonah was in the belly of the fish three days and three nights" (Jonah 1:17). The text teaches us that God not only appointed the means, but He also appointed the time. The fish swallowed Jonah because God appointed the fish. Jonah was in the belly of the fish three days and three nights because God appointed the time. As the psalmist says, "The course of my life is in your power" (Ps. 31:15). Jonah learned this truth.

Can you imagine Jonah down in that belly of the fish? Three days and three nights might seem like a brief time, but if you are in the belly of a fish at the bottom of the ocean, that would seem like an eternity.

You know what God was doing here? When God placed Jonah down into the belly of that fish, at the bottom of that sea, for three days and for three nights, God was once again confirming His appointment with Jonah. God said, "I told you, you have an appointment. Now you're going to sit here in the waiting room until I'm ready." For three days and three nights Jonah sat in the Lord's waiting room. And if you have ever been in a waiting room, then you know what it means to cry out, "How long?"

"How long, O Lord?" is the cry of those who have had to wait on the Lord. In Psalm 13:1 David says, "How long, LORD? Will you forget me forever? How long will you hide your face from me?" Again, in Psalm 35:17, he cries, "Lord, how long will you look on? Rescue me from their ravages; rescue my precious life from the young lions."

God determines how long you wait in His waiting room. God determines the times. God promised Abraham that he would have a seed, and he waited in God's waiting room twenty-five years. God appoints the times. Jacob had to wait fourteen years to marry Rachel. God appoints the times. Joseph languished in prison for three years for a crime he didn't commit. Why? Because God appoints the times in which you languish and wait in His waiting room. Moses spent forty years on the backside of the desert, outside of Egypt because God appoints the times. Like Jonah, Jesus was in the grave three days and three nights because God appoints the times. The days and times for Jonah in the service of God were not through.

Yet, there was the miracle in it all. The miracle is not that the fish swallowed Jonah. A big fish can do that. The miracle is that while he was in the fish he didn't see corruption. The miracle is that while he was in the fish for those three days and three nights he was not allowed to see decay. The grave did not overcome him. Acts 13:35 and 37 say that Jesus, whom God ordained, went down into death and the grave for three days and three nights, and did not see "decay"; the same was true here of Jonah.

This is an important reminder and encouragement to us. If you are a Christian, you may go down, but however long He sends you down, He will not let you go out.

Remember, it is God's appointed time. It is His appointed waiting room. God will not allow you to be swallowed up by death. Like Jesus and Jonah, He will not allow you to be consumed by the grave. If you are saved, this is a wonderful revelation. The Bible tells us that each of us has an appointment with God. Every human being upon the face of the earth has an appointment with God. Hebrews 9:27 says, "It is appointed for people to die once—and after this, judgment." An appointment is coming for every human being.

You are not going to get out of it, even if you think you are can outrun it. Sooner or later God will catch up to you and put you in His waiting room. For every person there is an appointed time. You have an appointment with God to die and then the judgment. The only question at that time is: Will He allow you to be consumed? If you are in Christ, then you will be like Jonah. God will not allow you to be corrupted. If you are in Christ, God will not allow death to overtake or overcome you. If you are in Christ, then just as God raised Christ from the dead, so is the promise to you—you too will be raised from the dead.

The Christian knows that there is a coming appointment with God, and the Christian doesn't run from it. Christians welcome the appointment with God because they know God will not allow death to win. Our lives are in His hands. Our times are in His hands. They are His appointed times according to His appointed means, to bring about His appointed ends.

Appointed Ends

Sooner or later God tracks us down. God appoints the time. God appoints the means. He has appointed the ends.

Consider this: God has appointed the means of salvation (perhaps the reading of this book). He has appointed the time (now is the time, and today is the day of salvation—2 Cor. 6:2). He has appointed the ends (the prayer of faith unto repentance). Perhaps today is the day you stop running. Perhaps today is the day you acknowledge your need for God. Perhaps today is the day you pray. When the appointed ends came, Jonah prayed. The text says, "Then Jonah prayed to the LORD his God from the belly of the fish: "I called to the LORD in my distress" (Jonah 2:1–2 ESV).

The appointed end to which God is bringing all of us is to acknowledge that He is God and we are not. There is one sovereign omnipotent God. He is Lord over all. Through the appointed means, at the appointed time, God brought Jonah to this appointed end. Jonah was reminded that God is God, and Jonah is not. And then Jonah prayed.

The Will of God: Prayer

The will of God will always get done—not yours, not mine, but God's will. And what is God's will? Part of God's will is that men and women pray. God brought Jonah to his knees. And that is where God delights to bring all of us. Jonah prayed.

He Prayed out of the Depths

The Bible says that Jonah prayed out of the depths. He prayed from the belly of the fish. He prayed out of the "belly of Sheol"—from the depths of the grave. Jonah had fallen to the lowest of lows, to the lowest depths, even to the grave. He had fallen to the depths of his sin. He had fallen and sunk to the depths of his disobedience. And out of the depths of his disobedience and sin, out of the depths of the grave, Jonah cried. He prayed like the psalmist:

> Out of the depths I call to you, LORD!
> Lord, listen to my voice;
> let your ears be attentive
> to my cry for help.
>
> LORD, if you kept an account of iniquities,
> Lord, who could stand?
> But with you there is forgiveness,
> so that you may be revered. (Ps. 130:1-4)

Here is the beautiful reminder that there is no place too low out of which you cannot cry out to God. There is no grave too dark or sea too deep out of which you cannot call upon God. In fact, only when it is dark enough for you to realize your helplessness and hopelessness do you really begin to see the stars of His mercy and His grace. It is out of those depths that Isaac Watts taught us to sing:

> *From deep distress and troubled thoughts*
> *To thee, my God, I raised my cries;*
> *If thou severely mark our faults,*
> *No flesh can stand before thine eyes.*
> *But thou hast built thy throne of grace*
> *Free to dispense thy pardons there*
> *That sinners may approach thy face,*
> *And hope and love, as well as fear.*[10]

He Prayed out of Distress

Out of the lowest parts of his sin and disobedience, Jonah cried out to God. He cried out from the depths. He not only cried out from the depths, but those depths brought him to distress, and he cried out of his distress. "I called to the LORD in my distress, and he answered me" (Jonah 2:2). Where was he? He was down in the depths of his disobedience, in the depths of his sin. While down there his heart was gripped by the distressing nature of the moment. He came to understand the direness of his situation.

You might remember earlier the captain of the boat came to Jonah and said, "What are you doing sound asleep? Get up! Call to your god" (Jonah 1:6). What did Jonah do? At the time he refused to pray. Yet once he found himself in the belly of the grave, he prayed. He prayed out loud! He prayed with fervency! He prayed with urgency! Jonah prayed!

Admittedly, most of us don't pray until we have nothing else to do but pray. That isn't ideal but better late than never. If you don't ever remember to pray until distressing circumstances come, then at least pray then. In fact, isn't it remarkable and an amazing demonstration of His grace that God even delights to answer seemingly late prayers?

Why would He answer Jonah then? Why would He answer you? You didn't pray before the trouble. You didn't pray while creating the problem. But now that you've created a huge mess, all of a sudden you want to call on God. Yet it is a testimony to God's grace and goodness that He answers prayers that are after the fact of our disobedience.

Someone has said, "I'm too blessed to be stressed." Well, you need to understand that sometimes the "blessed" comes in the middle of the "stressed" because in the distressing moments we learn to cry out to God. In God's bringing me into distressing situations, I'm reminded of my need and dependence on Him, and therefore I am able to find the blessing in the stressing.

And so it was with Jonah. He didn't cry out when he was above the water. Yet, when he got below the water, inside the belly of the fish, he cried out to his God. Thankfully, God says in Psalm 81:7, "You called out in distress, and I rescued you." And the psalmist says, "In my distress I called to the LORD, and he answered me" (Ps. 120:1).

What a blessing! Even though you may call on God late, it is never too late to call on God. If you have wind in your lungs, soundness in your mind, and a beat in your heart, then you can call on God. Yes, you should have prayed yesterday, but you can pray now. Yes, you should have repented yesterday, but you can and should repent now. "Yesterday's gone," the songwriter says, "and tomorrow may never be mine. Lord, help me today, show me the way one day at a time." Show me to pray today. Whatever happened yesterday is gone. And don't worry about tomorrow. Call on the Lord today, and find that it will be well with your soul.

Not only can you call on the Lord, but amazingly He is ready and willing to answer. Actually it is not amazing that sinners pray at times of distress. That's what we do. Someone has rightly said, "There are no atheists in foxholes." When things get tight and tough, everybody prays, "Lord, have mercy!" It is not amazing that sinners pray in distressing moments. What is amazing is that God delights to answer the prayers of these rebellious sinners. That's amazing! And that's what He does and what He will do for you this very day.

You may say, "But I've gone too far." Sure, things may have gone further than you intended for them to go. Things may be more distressing than they should be. Your disobedience has caused you and others pain and frustration. It's OK. If you pray out of your distress, God will delight to hear. He has not forsaken you.

God didn't allow Jonah to perish. You know what that fish was? That fish was the salvation of God. God sent salvation. That's why you don't focus on the fish; you focus on God. There was a great fish. Yes, but that's because there is a great God who sent the fish, which swooped up Jonah and saved him at the powerful command of God. So you see that the fish points us to the grace of God in Jesus Christ.

We might ask Jonah, "How were you saved, Jonah?"

Jonah would reply, "God sent a fish to swallowed me up, and set me once again on dry land."

You might ask me, "How were you saved, Tony?"

Similar to Jonah, I would reply, "He brought me up from a desolate pit, out of the muddy clay, and set my feet on a rock, making my steps secure" (Ps. 40:2).

The songwriter said it best:

> My heart was distressed 'neath Jehovah's dread
>   frown,
> And low in the pit where my sins dragged me
>   down;
> I cried to the Lord from the deep miry clay,
> Who tenderly brought me out to golden day.
>
> He brought me out of the miry clay,
> He set my feet on the Rock to stay;
> He puts a song in my soul today,
> A song of praise, hallelujah![11]

Today some might be tempted to say to Jonah, "Jonah, God loves you and has a wonderful plan for your life. In fact, He's going to throw you down to the bottom of the ocean and let a fish swallow you whole. He's going to keep you in the belly of that fish for three days and three nights (hard to miss all the smelly and disgusting contents of the fish), and have that fish vomit you back on dry land and say, 'Get back to preaching.'"

Jonah might say in return, "If that's the way He loves me and the wonderful plan He has for my life, you can miss me with that."

And we do miss it until we understand it's God's appointed means, and God's appointed times, to bring us to God's appointed ends. Don't miss it! Through divine appointments we come to realize our need for God. And we pray. And we trust His plan is wonderful and His love never-ending. And we pray, amen.

True Repentance
Jonah 2:1–10

———

Jonah prayed to the LORD his God from the belly of the fish:

I called to the LORD in my distress, and he answered me.
I cried out for help from deep inside Sheol;
you heard my voice. You threw me into the depths,
into the heart of the seas, and the current overcame me.
All your breakers and your billows swept over me.
But I said, "I have been banished from your sight,
yet I will look once more toward your holy temple.
The water engulfed me up to the neck;
the watery depths overcame me;
seaweed was wrapped around my head.
I sank to the foundations of the mountains,
the earth's gates shut behind me forever!
Then you raised my life from the Pit, LORD my God!
As my life was fading away, I remembered the LORD,
and my prayer came to you, to your holy temple.
Those who cherish worthless idols
abandon their faithful love,
but as for me, I will sacrifice to you
with a voice of thanksgiving.
I will fulfill what I have vowed.
Salvation belongs to the LORD."

Then the LORD commanded the fish, and
it vomited Jonah onto dry land.

I graduated from a college where some of the students believed in a doctrine called "baptismal regeneration." Baptismal regeneration is just a fancy theological term for the belief that a person is saved and receives the Holy Spirit at the moment that person is baptized. It is believed that through being immersed in water you receive the free gift of eternal life. In fact, some would go so far as to say that particular ministers must baptize you in a particular church for you to be saved.

Baptism is important. Therefore, we do seek to faithfully administer this biblical sacrament. We want to make sure we hold baptism in as high esteem as the Bible does. However, while baptism is important and is necessary for obedience to Christ, we need to understand that baptism is not essential to salvation. In fact, baptism is not essential to understanding and proclaiming the gospel of Jesus Christ. It is not essential to trusting in the gospel of Jesus Christ. The apostle Paul makes this point in 1 Corinthians, where he clearly states, "For Christ did not send me to baptize, but to preach the gospel" (1:17). Clearly the Bible draws a dichotomy between preaching the gospel and baptism. While baptism is important in the life of the disciple, and arguably the first act of obedience unto Christ, the gospel is clearly understood and believed before it.

However, while baptism is not essential to the gospel, some things are essential to faithful gospel proclamation and understanding. Some things, if you don't have them, you don't have the gospel. If you don't preach them, you don't preach the gospel. One of those necessities is the grace of repentance.

Repentance is essential to the gospel. The gospel is never faithfully proclaimed or understood apart from the call to repent. And you see this throughout the Scriptures, but particularly in the life and preaching ministry of Jesus and His disciples. Here are some examples:

John the Baptist

> "Repent, because the kingdom of heaven has come near." (Matt. 3:2)

Jesus

> From then on Jesus began to preach, "Repent, because the kingdom of heaven has come near." (Matt. 4:17)

The Disciples

> So they went out and preached that people should repent. (Mark 6:12)

Paul

> Having overlooked the times of ignorance,
> God now commands all people everywhere
> to repent. (Acts 17:30)

Jesus

> Remember then how far you have fallen;
> repent, and do the works you did at first.
> (Rev. 2:5)

The songwriter has it right. In calling men and women to Christ, he wrote:

> *Come, ye thirsty, come, and welcome,*
> *God's free bounty glorify;*
> *True belief and true repentance,*
> *Every grace that brings you nigh.*[12]

Amen! That's how you come nigh unto God—through faith and repentance.

Preaching the gospel always includes repentance. Those who faithfully proclaim the gospel of Jesus Christ not only call others to repent but also know the grace of repentance themselves. And so it was with Jonah.

God called Jonah to go to Nineveh and call the Ninevites to repentance. Jonah refused to do what God commanded him to do and, therefore, Jonah found himself in the predicament of being in the belly of a large fish at the bottom of the sea. What did God call Jonah to do there? That's right, repent.

Repentance

What is repentance? It is good and helpful for us to define the term. Simply put, repentance is godly sorrow. It is godly sorrow over our sin, coming from the conviction of the Holy Spirit, making us aware that we have offended God. Having this conviction, we desire to turn *from* sin and in obedience turn *to* God in our thoughts and actions. Wayne Grudem, in his *Systematic Theology*, defines *repentance* as "a sincere desire to forsake sin and walk in obedience to Christ."[13] The Westminster Shorter Catechism defines *repentance* as "a sinner, out of a true sense of his sin, and apprehension of the mercy of God in Christ, does with grief and hatred of his sin, turn from it unto God, with full purpose of, endeavor after, new obedience."[14] The common thread running through all those definitions is a forsaking of your sin. It is grieving over the sin that has offended God, but also turning from that sin into a full embrace of a new life of obedience unto God. In fact, this is what the prophecy of Jonah reveals to us.

The focus of the prophecy of Jonah is the need of human beings everywhere to repent before God. Unfortunately, most of the time when we look at the prophecy of Jonah, most of us focus on the fish. We focus our attention on questions like, Was it a whale? Is it possible that a human being can live three days in the belly of a fish and then be vomited on dry land? How big exactly was the fish? What else was swimming around in the whale's belly? Interestingly, the Bible doesn't make a big deal about the fish. It just says, "The LORD appointed a great fish" (Jonah 1:17), and it swallowed up Jonah.

Our fixation on the fish can cause us to miss the true message of Jonah. In fact, one writer and commentator confessed, "I was so obsessed with what was going inside the whale that I missed seeing the drama going on inside of Jonah."[15] Inside Jonah, the real drama was taking place. That is the focus of Scripture. Don't misunderstand. The fish is important, but the emphasis of Scripture is on Jonah and his repentance. And true repentance begins with *acknowledging your sin.*

Acknowledge Your Sin

Before God would use Jonah, God would bring Jonah to the end of himself. God brought Jonah to admit and confess, "I am a sinner." That's where true repentance begins. It is acknowledging that you are a sinner. It is acknowledging the main thing wrong with my world is me! It is acknowledging that your sin is the source of your misery. This is what Jonah came to understand.

Ask yourself the question, "Who's fault was it that Jonah was in the belly of the fish at the bottom of a sea?" It was Jonah's. This is the first step in repentance. You must acknowledge, "Lord, it's not my mother, it's not my sister, it's not my father, it's not my brother; Lord, it's me. I am the issue. I am the biggest hindrance to my coming to You. It's me."

Jonah realized this. Remember in chapter 1 when the sea was raging against the boat, the boat was tossed, and everything was going to be lost? Jonah told the men on the boat, "Throw me into the sea so that it will calm down" (Jonah 1:12). Why did he say that? Because he knew the reason for the storm. The misery they experienced was Jonah's fault. The men eventually threw Jonah overboard into the sea. Yet, once overboard and swallowed by the fish, Jonah realized that his new situation was not just from the men who had thrown him overboard, but it was the chastisement of

God for his sin. From the belly of the fish, Jonah cried out in prayer, "You threw me into the depths, into the heart of the seas" (2:3).

In other words, "You did this, God. You have done this for my chastisement because I have walked in disobedience—because of my sin. You have done this."

Jonah doesn't lay the blame at the feet of those who threw him overboard for the issues in his life or the misery he was experiencing. The chastisement was his at this moment. Those men were inconsequential in the grand scheme of things. God had done this. *Ultimately, your sin causes your misery.*

This idea of repentance is plainly stated for us in Psalm 38. The psalmist wrote, "There is no soundness in my body because of your indignation; there is no health in my bones because of my sin" (v. 3). Jonah echoed the psalmist. He knew why death was upon him. He knew the reason for his calamity. He knew why the waters had surrounded him and the weeds had wrapped around his head. He knew why things were happening. He knew the source of his misery.

Jonah went down into misery because he chose to go down into misery. No, he didn't get in that boat thinking he would end up in the belly of a fish at the bottom of the sea. That's not what he thought he was doing when he got into that boat. And yet the choice he made to live in disobedience to God was a choice that was ultimately headed toward the grave.

Most people don't think they are choosing misery when they choose to disobey God. In fact, they think they are choosing pleasure, fun, or self-fulfillment. But the end result is always the same. Jonah thought he was getting in that boat for a pleasure trip to Tarshish. Yet what he was really doing was living his life in disobedience to God. That trip to Tarshish was going nowhere fast. When you decide to disobey God and to live your life in rebellion, you decide to move away from God. When you decide to move away from God, your life is steadily on a downward spiral. If you belong to God, however, the Bible says your rebellion is a concern to God, and like a loving father, He is going to discipline you (Heb. 12:6).

When I was growing up, they used to tell us that "a hard head makes for a soft behind." That may not be true in our homes anymore. There are far too many hard heads and too few soft behinds. But it is still true with God. Hard heads do still make for soft behinds, and you see it here with Jonah. True repentance, therefore, understands that when God comes in chastisement for your disobedience, there are no more excuses.

King David understood this well. When David was confronted with his sin, he responded, "I am conscious of my rebellion, and my sin is always before me" (Ps. 51:3). Can you hear Jonah saying, "I'm in the belly of this fish because I am conscious of my rebellion, and my sin is always before me"? No more excuses. You have to take responsibility for your sin. That's the only way you get to true repentance. David did that. Jonah did that. But unfortunately, that's not our first instinct.

Pointing the Finger

Our first instinct is to blame others for our sin. We get this from our first parents, Adam and Eve. When Adam and Eve fell into sin in the garden of Eden, God came to them and asked, "Adam, where are you? Adam, what have you done?" Immediately, rather than taking responsibility for his sin, Adam replied, "It's the woman you gave me. It's her fault. If she hadn't been here, you wouldn't be asking me that question. If she hadn't talked to me and convinced me, then I would not have sinned. It's her fault." God then spoke to Eve, and Eve likewise blamed someone else, saying, "It's the serpent's fault. If you hadn't let him into this garden and given him access to us, then I wouldn't have sinned" (see Gen. 3:8-13). Our first instinct is to blame others. It's what we do, and we do it a lot.

God often uses other people to show us our sin. Our first instinct is to blame them. Consequently, our friends and families, whom God uses to show us our sin, suddenly become our enemies. We respond, "I don't like the way you talk to me. I don't like the way you said that. I don't like what you said."

I cannot tell you how many times I have sat down with couples and individuals for counsel, and before long I discover they don't want counsel; they want confirmation. They don't want counsel. They want me to confirm them in their sin. When I don't confirm them in their sin, I become the bad guy. Rather than their sin being on the chopping block, they want my head on the chopping block. But the counselor is not the problem. Sin is. Passing the blame won't bring resolution.

Jonah didn't blame those men for his trip to the bottom of that sea or for being in the belly of that fish. He knew it was his sin.

If you ever are inclined to go to someone for counsel, own your sin. That is the only way you're going to get to true repentance. You must own it. It's yours. Don't blame somebody else. Don't blame the one who points it out. Don't blame the one who tries to counsel you out of it. Instead say, I "have sinned and fallen short of the glory of God" (Rom. 3:23).

You see this illustrated for us in the Bible. In fact, it is the tale of two kings and the men of God who spoke to them. It is the interaction between King Herod and John the Baptist and between David and the prophet Nathan.

A *Tale of Two Kings*

In Mark 6, John the Baptist preached against King Herod because Herod was in an illicit relationship and was living in sin. John the Baptist spoke out publicly against Herod's indiscretions. And what did Herod do when he heard that John the Baptist was preaching against his sin? Did he repent of his sin? Did he get before God and say, "God, I have sinned against You, against the nation, and against Your commands?" No! Instead of repenting of his sin, the king cut off the head of the prophet who was calling him to repentance. Rather than doing away with his sin, Herod did away with John.

But consider King David. The Bible records David's fall into sin with and against Bathsheba and against her husband Uriah. David was guilty of adultery, conspiracy, and murder (2 Sam. 11). God sent the prophet Nathan to confront the king in chapter 12. In the presence of the king's court, Nathan spoke the famous convicting words, "[David,] you are the man!" (2 Sam. 12:7).

In the face of the public indictment, what did David do? Did he get mad with Nathan? Did he say, "Nathan, why are you putting my business on blast? Why are you bringing me up before all these people in this court and telling my business?" David didn't say any of that. He knew it was not Nathan's fault; it was his own.

David understood that Nathan was the grace of God in his life. If you have people in your life who love you enough to talk to you about your sin, don't cut them off. Don't shut them down. Don't blame them. They are the grace of God to you.

Rather than get rid of Nathan, David went before God and prayed, "Be gracious to me, God . . . ; blot out my rebellion. . . . wash me, and I will be whiter than snow. . . . let the bones you have crushed rejoice" (Ps. 51:1, 7–8).

True repentance is acknowledging your sin and knowing that your sin has caused your misery. However, it's not only knowing that your sin has caused your misery; it's also the conviction of your sin that points you to the mercy of God. That's why you want to acknowledge it. That's why you want to own it. Not only does it cause you misery, but in the misery of sin, you find the mercy of God. It's the only way.

From Misery to Mercy

Mercy is the goodness and compassion of God in the midst of misery. If you are not willing to acknowledge your misery, you won't experience God's mercy. You must be willing to acknowledge your misery and the sin that caused it. When you do, you will also realize that God is good and compassionate to sinners. In fact, your sin will then point you to Christ as you move from misery to mercy, just as it did for Jonah.

The mercy of God is transitional. It not only transforms our lives, but it transitions us as well. It transitions us from death to life. It transitions us from darkness to light.

Jonah said, "I have been banished from your sight, yet I will look once more toward your holy temple" (Jonah 2:4). Then again he said, "I sank to the foundations of the mountains, the earth's gates shut behind me forever! Then you raised my life from the Pit, LORD my God!" (2:6). The transitions are clear.

> "I have been banished from your sight, yet
> I will look once more toward your holy
> temple." (2:4, emphasis added)

"I sank to the foundations of the mountains,
the earth's gates shut behind me forever!
Then you raised my life from the Pit, LORD
my God!" (2:6, emphasis added)

The mercy of God transitions us and reminds us that because of the grace of repentance, sin is never the final word in the Christian life. *Yet* mercy comes.

When you acknowledge your sin, confess your sin, and own your sin, you then make a beeline to Christ. You run to Jesus. You run to the cross and find "mercy there was great, and grace was free; pardon there was multiplied to me."[16] But you have to acknowledge your sin. You have to own it. When you do, mercy will be yours.

How do we know Jonah received the mercy of God? The text tells us. We know he received the mercy of God because Jonah prayed. Notice what he said: "As my life was fading away, I remembered the LORD, and my prayer came to you" (2:7). Prayer is a mercy from God. It is a mercy because no one prays who is not first moved by God to do so. Crying out to God for mercy is the mercy of God upon your life, awakening you to your need of Him.

Consider this: What makes you aware of your sin? What makes you aware of your rebellion? What makes you aware of your disobedience? It is the grace and mercy of God.

What causes a person to cry out to God? What causes a person to truly get before God and repent of his sins? Is it not the mercy of God in the first place?

Most of us don't pray until we find ourselves in misery. And yet that should remind us that our misery is the grace of God causing us to cry out to God for mercy. Therefore, we can thank God for the misery because then we come to understand and know His mercy.

God delights to answer the prayer, "God, have mercy on me, a sinner!" (Luke 18:13). He always has. When you repent and need mercy, you will receive mercy. God delights to give it. However, when you refuse to repent and seek that which you need most, you forsake your greatest need—namely, the mercy and love of God. Accordingly, Jonah admitted, "Those who cherish worthless idols abandon their faithful love" (Jonah 2:8).

The Hebrew word translated as "faithful love" is *hesed*. It means "the mercy of God." It means "the covenant faithfulness of God." It is the loving-kindness of God, whereby God is merciful to sinners.

Jonah said, "Those who cherish." In other words, those who worship, those who give their attention to vain and worthless idols, forsake the hope of mercy they so desperately need.

We all have idols. Tim Keller reminds us that "idols are spiritual addictions."[17] They cause us to break the rules, to violate the law, and to harm others and even ourselves, to get to them.[18] "An idol," Keller writes, "is anything more important to you than God, anything that absorbs your heart and imagination more than God, anything you seek to give you what only God can give you is an idol."[19]

We all have idols—money, popularity, sex, self, power, influence, friends, family members. The list goes on and on. Any of these can become idols when we pay closer attention to them than we do to the worship of God. The question is not whether you and I have idols. Rather, the question is, are we turning from them in repentance? The only cure for spiritual addiction is the mercy of God. It's the steadfast love, the covenant faithfulness of God. God's mercy is the only cure.

Interestingly, an instrument God sometimes uses to help cure spiritual addictions is the same one used to help cure drug addictions—interventions.

When it comes to addictions, interventions often work. This is what Jonah received. Jonah received a spiritual intervention. This is what David received. This is what the apostle Paul received on the road to Damascus. Spiritual interventions are often God's way of reminding us not to take the mercy of God lightly. Sometimes the interventions are dramatic, like David and Paul. Other times it is through the ordinary means of grace.

For example, every week you go to church and you hear the Word of God sung, and you hear the Word of God preached, that is God intervening in your life, saying, "Wake up! Don't forsake the mercy of God to you this morning. Wake up! Don't just acknowledge your sin, but wake up! and acknowledge your Savior." Acknowledge Him who has come to save you. Acknowledge Him who has come to show you the mercy of God. At the heart of every spiritual intervention from God is the blessed, beloved Savior. Acknowledge Him.

Acknowledge the Savior

That's why you shouldn't get upset about the intervention. Instead, drop the addiction and look to Christ. That's what Jonah did. He was down in the fish for three days when the spiritual intervention came to him. Suddenly the light came on, and he not only acknowledged his sin, but then he acknowledged his Savior. Those who are made aware of their sin are then made aware also that there is only one hope, and that hope is Jesus.

There is only one hope, and Jonah expressed this in a sentence that is one of the most blessed words in the Bible:

"Salvation belongs to the LORD!" (Jonah 2:9 ESV). Jonah finally got it. He woke up. "Salvation belongs to the LORD!" (We should note the exclamation point for emphasis in the English Standard Version.) This is where God was bringing Jonah—to the point where he would acknowledge, "Salvation is of the LORD!" The New Living Translation adds an "alone" to make the emphasis: "For my salvation comes from the LORD alone." The glorious and gracious truth was clear to Jonah. It should be clear to us as well. Salvation is of the Lord alone!

True repentance demands trust in Christ. It demands seeing that salvation comes no other way but through Jesus. To say that salvation belongs to the Lord is to say what the Bible says elsewhere: "from him and through him and to him are all things" (Rom. 11:36). To say that salvation belongs to the Lord is to say that salvation is "from him," that salvation is "through him," that salvation is "to him"!

Salvation Is from Him

He is "the source and perfecter of our faith" (Heb. 12:2). Christ brings salvation to us. It's from the Lord. Our minds did not conceive it. Our hands did not bring it to pass. Our feet do not keep us in it. Salvation belongs to the Lord!

We often hear people make the statement, "We need to have a come-to-Jesus meeting." Actually, you don't come to Jesus; He comes to you. He comes to you, and in coming to you, you are allowed to come to Him. That's what we celebrate at Christmastime—salvation came down. Jesus came to us. Read the Scriptures, and you will find that many people came to Jesus while Jesus was on the earth. Yet, if you look closely, it's actually Jesus who made Himself available to them. You don't come to Jesus unless Jesus first comes to you. And when He comes, He says, "Come to me" (Matt. 11:28), because salvation is from the Lord.

Salvation Is through Him

Contrary to popular opinions, all dogs do not go to heaven; nor do all roads lead there. There is only one way—it is through the Lord. Salvation is not a smorgasbord. Repentance is not like Golden Corral. God's Word is clear: "There is no other name under heaven given to people by which we must be saved" (Acts 4:12). There is only one way. That's why, when it comes to preaching the gospel, the preacher has one message: "Jesus Christ and him crucified" (1 Cor. 2:2). Salvation is through Christ alone. Consequently, when it comes to our message, the church of Jesus Christ is a one-trick pony. Jesus Christ is the only way.

Salvation Is to Him

Salvation does not come to us in order to make much of us. God doesn't save us to make us great. He saves so that we will know how great He is. Salvation honors Him. Salvation brings Him glory and praise. Salvation is not about us, and neither is our repentance. Jonah learned it wasn't about him; salvation is about God. Salvation belongs to God.

You know what happened to Jonah in that fish? Jonah had a come-to-Jesus moment. And yet he realized that the only reason he could come to Jesus was because in the midst of his misery, Jesus came to him. And that's why Jonah could sing, as we can sing,

> *I heard the voice of Jesus say, "Come unto me*
> *and rest;*
> *Lay down, thou weary one, lay down, thy head*
> *upon my breast."*
> *And I came to Jesus just as I was, wounded,*
> *weary and sad;*
> *And I found in him a resting-place, and he has*
> *made me glad.*[20]

Gladness comes from true repentance. That's the end goal. When you truly repent, your heart is made glad. You are no longer burdened with that sin and transgression. You are free to worship God in spirit and in truth. Repentance and gladness are God's desire for us. All those who trust in Christ are heirs of His joy and gladness. There is no sin too great that our Lord will not forgive or burden too heavy for Him to make you glad if you would come to Him. Come, come to Jesus. He has come to you.

Redemption

Jonah 3:1–10

———

The word of the LORD came to Jonah a second time: "Get up! Go to
the great city of Nineveh and preach the message that I tell you." Jonah
got up and went to Nineveh according to the LORD's command.

Now Nineveh was an extremely great city, a three-day walk.
Jonah set out on the first day of his walk in the city and proclaimed, "In forty days Nineveh will be demolished!" Then the
people of Nineveh believed God. They proclaimed a fast and
dressed in sackcloth—from the greatest of them to the least.

When word reached the king of Nineveh, he got up from
his throne, took off his royal robe, put on sackcloth, and
sat in ashes. Then he issued a decree in Nineveh:

By order of the king and his nobles: No person or animal, herd or
flock, is to taste anything at all. They must not eat or drink water.
Furthermore, both people and animals must be covered with sackcloth,
and everyone must call out earnestly to God. Each must turn from his
evil ways and from his wrongdoing. Who knows? God may turn and
relent; he may turn from his burning anger so that we will not perish.

God saw their actions—that they had turned from their
evil ways—so God relented from the disaster he had
threatened them with. And he did not do it.

Have you ever found yourself being pursued? Perhaps it was as innocent as a game of hide-and-seek. Or perhaps it was as intense as having law enforcement and the police on your trail. The sense of being pursued and chased can be an unsettling experience.

Those who study such things tell us that some of the most common and distressing dreams people have are what are known as "chase dreams"—a dream in which you are being chased or pursued by something or someone who has the intention of doing you harm. Experts tell us that chase dreams are actually the source of many sleepless nights and much anxiety in many people. When God is in pursuit of you, however, it is not a dream.

When God determines to pursue you, it's time to wake up. Many can testify to the sense of being pursued and hounded by God. In fact, my own conversion story, in part, is the story of finally realizing that God was in pursuit of me. He brought me to the end of myself in showing me the vanity of my ways and the futility of my life in running from Him.

However, when God pursued me, it wasn't to do me harm but good, because His pursuit was unto my redemption. Jesus says, "For the Son of Man has come to seek and to save the lost" (Luke 19:10). When God seeks, He seeks to save. He does that for our good. It has always been the case.

After Adam and Eve sinned, God sought them. They thought He was coming to do them harm, but ultimately God sought them to do them good. When God sought after Noah, He came to Noah not to harm Noah but to save him. When He came to Abraham, He came not to do Abraham harm but to save him. When Jesus sought after Peter, He sought after Peter to redeem and save him. When Jesus pursued Paul on the road to Damascus, He pursued Paul unto redemption. This was the case with Jonah. God pursued Jonah unto his redemption and the redemption of Nineveh.

Redemption

What is redemption? The simplest definition is that redemption is freedom. To be redeemed is to be set free by a power greater than the one that has held you captive. This is wonderfully illustrated for us in the Old Testament, particularly as God is seen as redeeming the nation of Israel out of slavery in Egypt. As the Bible clearly states, "Remember that you were a slave in the land of Egypt and the LORD your God redeemed you" (Deut. 15:15). Redemption is freedom. God set Israel free from Egypt and thus redeemed them. Redemption is being set free by a power greater than the power that holds you captive.

Israel's redemption from Egypt points to our redemption in Christ. Like Israel, before Christ, we were slaves to sin (John 8:34; Rom. 6:20). We were held captive by sin. We were in bondage to sin. Jesus, the sacrificial Lamb of God, redeemed us by His blood (Eph. 1:7). He set us free because His blood is more powerful than the sin that enslaved us.

When God pursues us, He pursues us to set us free. Therefore, we need God to pursue us. We want God to pursue us. Before I was married, I pursued my wife, Adriane. I went after her in every way. I pursued Adriane unto marriage because I believed I needed her. I believed she would be good for me, and she is.

However, God doesn't pursue us because He needs us. God pursues us because we need Him. Therefore, you want Him to pursue you. You need Him to pursue you. He doesn't pursue you because it's good for Him, He pursues you because it is good for you. That's why He comes. That's why He pursued Jonah. God's pursuit of Jonah was unto Jonah's redemption, which was unto the redemption of Nineveh. This is the theme of Jonah 3—redemption. Admittedly, it's not the fullest picture of redemption in the Bible. The Bible would have us know more about redemption. Still, we can learn three important truths about redemption from Jonah. The first is that redemption is a second chance.

Redemption Is a Second Chance

"The word of the LORD came to Jonah a second time" (Jonah 3:1). Here is evidence of God's amazing grace in the life of His people. A second time assumes a first, and yet the first time does not guarantee a second. Amazingly, here we are taught that our God is a God of second chances.

America prides itself on being a country of second chances. Every time somebody gets into some bit of hot water, a public figure has a fall, the first thing Americans want to say is, "You know, everybody deserves a second chance." It is said so frequently, and universally affirmed, that you would think it was written into the Constitution. "Life, liberty, the pursuit of happiness, and a second chance." Well, that may be the way of the United States, but second chances are not guaranteed in the Bible. Lot's wife didn't get a second chance (Gen. 19:26). Uzzah, when he put his hand upon the ark of the covenant, didn't get a second chance (2 Sam. 6:7). Ananias, when he lied to Peter and the Holy Spirit, did not get a second chance (Acts 5:5). Second chances are not guaranteed; therefore, they are most illustrative of the grace of God in many ways.

Second chances are undeserved. No one is assured or guaranteed a do-over. Amazingly, Jonah got a do-over. God didn't discard Jonah after Jonah rebelled, though God could have. God could have left Jonah dead in the fish and moved on to the next person to accomplish His will. But Jonah got a do-over. Someone has said that being a grandparent is the ultimate do-over. We often witness bad parents who become good grandparents. As wonderful as it is, being a grandparent isn't the ultimate do-over. The ultimate do-over is redemption.

Consider today how your sin is wearing on you. If you are honest, you are uniquely and acutely aware of the sin you have committed, are committing, and are planning to commit. Yet God, even knowing all this, offers you a second chance. Jesus came not to condemn you (John 3:17) but to give you another chance. You might say, "Well, I have already used up my second chance." Then He is willing to give you a third chance. You say, "I have used up my third chance." Then He is going to give you a fourth chance. You may have used your fifth, tenth, or fiftieth chance, and yet the Lord is willing to give you another, and another, and another chance. He is not simply the God of the second chance; He is the God of another chance, and another. William Banks makes this point when he writes:

> We are moved to speak of Jonah's God as the God of the second chance. But honest sober reflection compels the saint to speak of Him

as the God of the 999th chance! Such gracious mercy as was extended to Jonah here,
and to David, and to the thief dying upon
the cross, and to Peter—surely it has been
granted to all believers through the precious
blood of Jesus Christ.[21]

As long as you have breath in your lungs and a beating
heart, you have another chance. In the grace and forgiveness of God, you can have a do-over! When I was a young
boy growing up in church, the offertory song was the same
week by week. The lyrics were simple: "You can't beat God's
giving, no matter how hard you try."[22] I often thought about
those words and would say to myself, *That's not very good
motivation for giving.* If I can't beat God giving no matter how
hard I try, maybe I should just stop trying. Interestingly,
however, the Bible does remind us that our sin can't outrace
the grace of God, no matter how hard we try. Your sin is not
greater than the grace of God, no matter how hard you try.

The Bible teaches us that where sin increases, grace
increases all the more (Rom. 5:20). No matter how great the
sin, the grace of God is greater. I know it may sound strange,
but in an ironic and yet glorious way, your sin magnifies the
grace of God. Sin is great; grace is greater still. It may be
hard to get our minds around that truth, but that's because

it's hard for us to grasp the power, love, and magnitude of the gospel of Jesus Christ.

So here is something even greater to understand. Indeed, your sin may magnify the grace of God, but your repentance and turning away from sin magnify it even more.

Romans 6 teaches us that greater than the grace that increases because of sin is the grace that empowers us to repent, turn from sin, and live faithfully unto Christ. The grace of a do-over is the matchless grace of God. How often have I heard people say, after being sinned against, "I forgive, but I won't forget." I often hear Christians say it. Isn't it good news and gracious news that God doesn't deal with us the way we deal with one another?

O. Palmer Robertson rightly summarizes God's words to Jonah. According to Robertson, God said, "Jonah, let's go at it again. . . . Jonah, let's start from the first. Let's forget the past and act as though it never happened."[23] This is the grace of a second chance. Every morning you should hear God saying, "Let's forget about last night. Yesterday is gone. Today there are new mercies and the Lord your God is faithful to forgive and forget" (see Lam. 3:22–23). This is the God of the second chance.

A second chance is that "in Christ, God was reconciling the world to himself, not counting their trespasses against them" (2 Cor. 5:19). Wow! That's the God of a second chance. That's the grace of God that is undeserved.

The word that came to Jonah the second time was not only undeserved, but it was also unchanged. It was identical to the word that came the first time. "Get up! Go to the great city of Nineveh and preach the message that I tell you" (Jonah 3:2). That's the same message as when God came to Jonah the first time. This is a sober reminder to us that God's Word does not change. If Jonah was counting on the word of God being different the second time around, he was sorely mistaken.

When we are confronted by the Word of God, we are often not particularly enthused by what it says. Therefore, we will frequently look around and seek a second opinion. We'll seek to find somebody who is willing to tell us, "Well, you know the Word of God really doesn't say that." They tell us that God has grown up and matured from such antiquated notions as found in the Scriptures. Yet the principle to remember is that because God does not change (Mal. 3:6), and His Word does not change.

If today the Word of God says children are to obey their parents, tomorrow the Word of God is going to say that children are to obey their parents. If today the Word of God says you are not to marry an unbeliever, tomorrow the Word of God is going to say you are not marry an unbeliever. If today the Word of God says not to cheat on your taxes, tomorrow the Word of God is going to say not to cheat on your taxes. If today the Word of God says salvation is by grace through faith in Christ alone, tomorrow the Word of God is going say that salvation is by grace through faith in Christ alone. The Bible testifies to its own immutability. "The grass withers, the flowers fade, but the word of our God remains forever" (Isa. 40:8).

The Word of God did not change; Jonah changed. God was the same. His word was the same. Jonah was different. The first time Jonah heard the word of the Lord to go to Nineveh, he fled in the other direction. The next time he heard the word of the Lord, he obeyed. He followed after God. The difference comes not in the Word; the difference must come in you and me.

In every church gathered in this world today, people are either changing the gospel, or the gospel is changing them. One or the other is happening. Either the gospel message is transforming lives, or people are deforming the gospel message. We must not seek to change God's Word but seek to be changed by it. Jonah was. And the whole city of Nineveh was as well. When the Word of God changes you, there is real change. Redemption is not just lip service. Redemption is head, heart, and hands service.

Redemption Changes Heads, Hearts, and Hands

When Jonah went to Nineveh, he did what God commanded him to do: he preached. He preached the righteous judgment of God against sin. He preached the necessity of repentance toward God. When the people of Nineveh heard the word of God proclaimed, the Bible says, "Then the people of Nineveh believed God" (Jonah 3:5). It seems really simple: "Oh, they believed God." It is the simplest thing God asks of us, and yet it is the most difficult thing to do.

All God ever asks of His people is to believe Him. And yet the thing we struggle with most is just that. The people of Nineveh believed God, and we see it in in their heads, we see it in their hearts, and we see it in their hands.

We see repentance in the Nineveites' heads in that they changed their minds about God, and they changed their minds about themselves. To believe and trust in God means we must stop believing and trusting in ourselves. We repent of self-lordship and submit to God's lordship.

This turning starts in the mind. The Bible says, "Do not be conformed to this age, but be transformed by the renewing of your mind" (Rom. 12:2). Repentance involves renewing the mind. It means we no longer trust the ways of the world. It means we trust in God's Word and think God's way. That's why the Bible encourages us to "adopt the same attitude as that of Christ Jesus" (Phil. 2:5). The idea is to think like God thinks—to have your mind infused with God's Word so that you can think like God thinks. Consequently, you think about sin like God thinks about sin. You think about Christ like God thinks about Christ. You think about yourself as God thinks about you.

That's what it means to believe God. God says, "You're a sinner," and you then believe and confess, "Lord, I am a sinner." God says, "Yes, but you are saved and justified by faith," and you respond, "Yes, Lord, I'm saved and justified by faith." God says, "You are holy; now walk in the newness of life," and you reply, "Yes, Lord, I'm going to walk in that holiness You have given to me." It is believing God. It's changing your mind and seeking to understand yourself and the world as God understands it.

Still, it is not only head; it's also heart. In other words, the Ninevites, in repenting, demonstrated affections for God above all other things. The Bible says they "believed God" and then they fasted (Jonah 3:5). In fact, the king, when he got word of it, issued a decree for no one, man or beast, to eat or drink anything, but to turn to God in repentance (vv. 7–8).

What is fasting? Fasting is an attempt to reorient our desires. There is nothing in this world that we desire more than food or drink. There is no greater impulse than the impulse to eat and drink. Perhaps you are eating or drinking as you read this book. Even as I write, I just finished eating lunch. When we are thirsty, our mouths become dry. When we are hungry, our stomachs growl, our hands shake, and our nerves get on edge. When it comes to food and water, no matter how young or old, we have to have it! Fasting is denying yourself food and drink for the purpose of saying, "There is nothing, God, I desire more than You. Nothing pulls at my affections more than You. Not even the most common desire for food and drink." It says, "Lord, I want You even more."

Such Godward affections are commended to us in Scriptures:

> As a deer longs for flowing streams, so I long for you, God. I thirst for God, the living God. (Ps. 42:1–2)

> Whom do I have in heaven but you? And I desire nothing on earth but you. My flesh and my heart may fail, but God is the strength of my heart, my portion forever. (Ps. 73:25–26)

The psalms are clear. There is no food, or water, or anything to be desired more than God. A mind renewed is also a heart with affections reoriented toward God. When we think God's thoughts, our hearts swell up with desire for Him above all others. Consequently, redeemed heads and redeemed hearts lead to redeemed hands. How do you know that what is in the head has gotten down into the heart? You look at the hands.

The king said, "Each must turn from his evil ways and from his wrongdoing" (3:8). In other words, don't just fast. Don't just say you believe, but show it by giving up your evil ways and the violence that is manifested in our land. That's how you know you've been redeemed. It shows in the lives we live. Those who think rightly about God and have right affections toward God seek to live their lives to the glory of God in righteousness, holiness, and truth.

True repentance, beloved, is not just what you say with your mouth. It really is what you do with your hands. The Bible says, "Faith, if it doesn't have works, is dead. . . . Show me your faith without works, and I will show you faith by my works" (James 2:17–18). That which you say you believe, and you confess and desire, must be manifested in the life you live.

This is how you know true repentance has taken hold. It's not simply that you say you're sorry or ask for forgiveness. It is that you begin to live a life contrary to the one you lived before. For example, the Bible says the repentant thief must not steal anymore. Instead, he is also called upon to work with his own hands, giving to others rather than taking (Eph. 4:28). The repentant hands match the repentant head and heart.

Wonderfully, the Ninevites repented at the word of Jonah. Yet, for us, One "greater than Jonah" has appeared (Luke 11:32). Jesus Christ is the Word of God at which we repent. And when we repent, we have full redemption. The Bible reminds us, "In him we have redemption through his blood, the forgiveness of our trespasses, according to the riches of his grace" (Eph. 1:7). In other words, my head has been redeemed, my heart has been redeemed, and my hands have been redeemed. This redemption is not by futile, empty things but by the precious blood of Christ. That's why we sing,

> *Redeemed, how I love to proclaim it!*
> *Redeemed by the blood of the Lamb.*
> *Redeemed by His infinite mercy,*
> *His child and forever I am.*[24]

My head, my heart, and my hands have been redeemed. Redemption is the whole person.

Redemption Is God Relenting

When men and women repent, God relents.

The king commanded his people to fast and pray because, as he said, "Who knows? God may turn and relent; he may turn from his burning anger so that we will not perish" (Jonah 3:9). The king knew what was at stake. He knew judgment of God was not simply Jonah selling wolf tickets. The judgment of God was real. Therefore, he threw himself and his nation upon the mercy of God, hoping and believing that if they repented and turned from their evil ways, who knows, God may be merciful. God didn't have to be, but He just may be merciful and relent from His fierce anger and from the terror He said would come upon them.

The Bible says, "God saw their actions—that they had turned from their evil ways—so God relented from the disaster he had threatened them with. And he did not do it" (v. 10). That is an amazing verse of Scripture. It raises the questions: Did God suddenly change His mind? Was God caught in a conundrum? Was God suddenly saying, "Oh my, they repented. Oh my! What am I going to do now?" They are legitimate and important questions. The answer to the question, "Did God change His mind?" is yes and no.

The answer is yes because that's what the text says. The text says God changed His mind. The text says, "God relented" (in the King James Version, "God repented"). The text says, "God relented from the disaster" He said would come upon them. God heard and saw them cry for mercy and responded in grace by relenting from the destruction. In that sense, God changed His mind. When the Ninevites changed their minds, God changed His.

This is important for us to realize. God is not disinterested in who we are and what we do. The Bible communicates God to us as active and not static. He is alive and engaged with His creation. As it moves, He moves. As it responds, He responds. He is not detached. His hand is upon this world, and He is shaping it and us, even as we shape our world.

Nevertheless, Nineveh's repentance was God's intended purpose from the beginning. This was why God sent Jonah in the first place. If God did not intend for the Ninevites to repent, He would not have sent Jonah.

Jonah was sent with the message of the gospel because God intended for the Ninevites to repent. As Jesus once reminded His disciples, "I have other sheep that are not from this sheep pen; I must bring them in also, and they will listen to my voice" (John 10:16). Here in Jonah is the message God has intended from the beginning: that the Gentile nations would be brought into the glories of the kingdom of God. Does God change His mind about the Gentiles? No! But then again, yes!

He changed His mind as far as Jonah and the Ninevites were concerned. He changed His mind as far as we can read and understand because God desires for those whom He redeems to know the awesome and terrible judgment from which they have been redeemed. He wants us to know it. He wants us to know the terrors of hell and judgment. He wants us to know the terrors of an eternal existence apart from His grace and His mercy. He wants us to know the awful and terrible condition of our souls if we refuse to repent.

Consequently, in your repentance you might get the understanding that God changed His mind about your judgment. You understand what a sweet and awful place it is in the mercy of God. But did God change His mind? The Ninevites might have thought so, and Jonah may have thought so, and you and I may think so, and that's OK. But God knows He didn't change His mind because God does not need to change His mind. He knows all things. "God is not a man, that he might lie, or a son of man, that he might change his mind" (Num. 23:19). That's what the Bible says. God doesn't need to change His mind. He knows the beginning from the end and the end from the beginning because He has ordained all things, even your repentance. From before He laid the foundations of the earth, God planned the redemption of the Ninevites.

God knows what Jonah doesn't know. God knows what the Ninevites don't know. God knows what you and I don't know. God knows not only the ends, but He knows the means by which the ends come. What does that mean? It means this: He not only knew that the Ninevites would be redeemed, but He also knew it would come through the preaching of Jonah.

Consider this: God not only knows who's going to heaven, but He also knows the means through which each of us is going to get there because He has gloriously ordained it all. That's why He can say, "I, the LORD, have not changed" (Mal. 3:6). God didn't change His mind about sin. He didn't change His mind about Jonah's sin, the Ninevites', your sin, or mine. He doesn't. He won't. He can't change His mind about sin. All sin must be punished. God didn't change His mind about sin. But instead of punishing us for our sin, instead of punishing Jonah, instead of punishing the Ninevites, He punished His Son, Jesus Christ, on the cross.

The Ninevites were redeemed and forgiven for the same reason you and I are. God took their sin and placed it on Jesus. He didn't change His mind; He only changed the recipient of His wrath. Once it was the Ninevites; then it was Jesus. Once it was you and me; now it's Jesus. Speaking of the substitution of Jesus for us, the prophet wrote: "He was pierced because of our rebellion, crushed because of our iniquities; punishment for our peace was on him, and we are healed by his wounds" (Isa. 53:5). Like Jonah and the Ninevites, we have been redeemed, restored, and forgiven.

The king of Nineveh hoped God would be merciful. In Jesus Christ the mercy of God is assured. We call upon God concerning many things. We call on Him to heal physical or emotional afflictions. We call on him to restore our finances or relationships. For these, and many others, we call on God in all sincerity, and still He may not be pleased to grant our requests. However, I guarantee you God will always grant one prayer. It is the prayer of the tax collector in Luke 18:13. It is the prayer for mercy. All those who ask the Lord our God for mercy will receive it. The Scriptures are quick to remind us that the character and heart of God are merciful. God delights to pardon and forgive sin: "Who is a God like you, forgiving iniquity and passing over rebellion for the remnant of his inheritance? He does not hold on to his anger forever because he delights in faithful love" (Mic. 7:18).

No matter who you are, where you have been, or what you have done, God is willing and ready to receive you. When you come to Him seeking mercy and pardon, you will discover that He is not angry. On the contrary, He is full of goodness and mercy for you.

Pursued by Love

Let the hide-and-seek be over. Francis Thompson's life came to a tragic end. We can only speculate as to the state of his mind and how he understood a gracious, loving, yet persistent God pursuing him through his nights and days. Yet we know from Thompson's great poem that he understood that the God who pursued him was the God who sought to do him good. This is a wonderful truth we see tragically, yet inspiringly demonstrated in the words of "The Hound of Heaven." In quoting God, Thompson wrote:

> And human love needs human meriting:
> How hast thou merited—
> Of all man's clotted clay the dingiest clot?
> Alack, thou knowest not
> How little worthy of any love thou art!
> Whom wilt thou find to love ignoble thee,
> Save Me, save only Me?[25]

In referencing "The Hound of Heaven," Michael Card wrote a song by the same name in which he said:

> *The dark and gloom you said*
> *You could no longer stand*
> *Was after all the shadow of My loving hand*
> *How little worthy of My love could anyone be*
> *Who else could ever love you, save only Me?*[26]

God pursued Thompson for Thompson's redemption. We can only hope that Thompson came to realize it. God pursued Jonah for Jonah's redemption and the redemption of the Ninevites. This is why God lovingly pursues you as well. Jonah and the Ninevites realized it. I pray you realize it too.

6

Jonah's Resentment, God's Restraint
Jonah 4:1–4

Jonah was greatly displeased and became furious. He prayed to the LORD: "Please, LORD, isn't this what I thought while I was still in my own country? That's why I fled toward Tarshish in the first place. I knew that you are a gracious and compassionate God, slow to anger, abounding in faithful love, and one who relents from sending disaster. And now, LORD, take my life from me, for it is better for me to die than to live."

The LORD asked, "Is it right for you to be angry?"

Arguably the most well-known parable our Lord Jesus ever told is the parable of the prodigal son. Few people, inside or outside the church, at the mention of the prodigal son would not be familiar with the parable or story that is given to us by Jesus in Luke 15. In the parable our Lord gives a powerful illustration of repentance and redemption. It is a story of a father's love and a wayward child. It is the story of forgiveness and celebration. It is a story both familiar and heartwarming. And yet it is also a sad story. It is a sad story of resentment.

It is a story of the resentment a son has for his father. The parable illustrates the resentment a brother could sadly have against his own brother and his father's choice to forgive that brother. The story of the prodigal son is an unforgettable tale and has found its indelible place among the pantheon of great lessons of the world. Jesus first told the parable in Luke 15, and yet the elements of the story are found in the Old Testament, namely in the life of the prophet Jonah. Before the father and his two sons in Luke 15, there was God, Jonah, and the Ninevites.

In a sense what we see in the prophecy of Jonah is a loving Father (God), a repentant son (the Ninevites), and a resentful older brother (Jonah). While the entire prophecy reminds us of God the loving Father and chapter 3 focuses our attention on the repentant son, the beginning of chapter 4 points us to the resentful brother. Yet, even in the face of unwarranted resentment, we see the loving restraint of God.

Chapter 4 begins with these words: "Jonah was greatly displeased and became furious" (v. 1). Naturally the question we should ask ourselves is, "What displeased Jonah?" The answer is found in chapter 3. It was the repentance of Nineveh coupled with the gracious relenting of God. The two of these together displeased Jonah and made him exceedingly angry.

God had used Jonah to bring about great revival among the people of Nineveh. Rather than rejoicing in what God did, the Bible says Jonah was vexed, greatly vexed in his soul. What the people of Nineveh did in response to his preaching displeased the prophet. What God did in response to what the people of Nineveh did displeased the prophet even more. Jonah considered what God did in forgiving the Ninevites to be offensive and a great evil.

Nineveh was a great city. It was the capital city of the Assyrian Empire. The Assyrians, at the time of Jonah, were known as vicious people. According to scholars:

> The Assyrians cultivated and earned a reputation as cruel barbarians (Isa. 10:12–15). Assyrian kings boasted of their military might and harsh treatment of those they

defeated, impaling their victims on spiked poles, burning cities, and carrying off much booty.[27]

Today we would call them terrorists. Assyria was a terrorist nation, and it terrorized all of its neighbors. Jonah and all of Israel wanted the Assyrians destroyed, and who can blame them? If God had moved in destruction against the Assyrians, against the Ninevites, no one would have lost any sleep because no one cries when the wicked get their just desserts.

Who in the church cried when Saddam Hussein was executed? Who in the church lost any sleep when the United States finally cornered Osama Bin Laden? Dare I say that no one cried when the Wicked Witch of the East or the White Witch of Narnia finally came to her demise? We feel this way because the wicked should be destroyed, right? Yet sometimes the wicked are not.

Instead of destroying the wicked, sometimes God redeems them. Sometimes God defeats the wicked not by destroying them but by extending grace to them and thus changing them. And what should be the response of God's people when God is pleased to redeem the wicked? Well, Jonah's response was resentment. He hated it.

Jonah's Resentment

Resentment is the feeling of anger or frustration at a real or perceived wrong or grievance. Jonah's anger and frustration at what God did for the Ninevites gave way to his expression of resentment as he spoke to God. He prayed to God, and it was not a prayer of submission, but rather it was a prayer in which he was seeking to justify himself, to vindicate himself, and to vilify God. In his prayer he resented Nineveh's repentance. It displeased him. He was not happy with the Ninevites, nor was he happy with God. He had hoped the Ninevites would not repent and God would destroy them.

Jonah wanted his enemies destroyed, not redeemed (see Jer. 18:20–21). Like the older brother in the parable of the prodigal son, Jonah didn't want his younger brothers to be forgiven. And like the older brother, Jonah resented when they returned to God. He resented the repentance of Nineveh. He resented God's forgiveness.

Yet he not only resented the repentance of Nineveh; he also resented his calling. Jonah said to God, "This is why I fled to Tarshish in the first place. This is the reason I fled from the call You had on my life." Jonah knew God might save the people of Nineveh, and he wanted no part of it. He knew this might happen, and apparently he made this objection known to God previously because he said, "Is this not what I said when I was yet in my country? Did I not say this would happen? Did I not say that You would forgive these wicked people? Did I not say that You would restrain Your hand from cutting them off the face of the earth? Did I not say You would do that?" (see Jonah 4:2).

God's agenda was not Jonah's agenda, and Jonah wanted no part of God's agenda. God's agenda was revival. Jonah didn't want it. God's agenda was repentance, and Jonah didn't want it. God's agenda was rejoicing, and Jonah wouldn't have it. Never mind that the Bible says we are to "rejoice with those who rejoice" (Rom. 12:15); Jonah didn't want to rejoice with the Ninevites. God had used him to bring joy to the hearts of others, and yet there was no joy in him. Like the older brother in the parable of the prodigal son, Jonah could think only of himself. He resented Nineveh's repentance, he resented his own calling by God, and, consequently, he resented God's grace.

Jonah remarked, "I knew that you are a gracious and compassionate God, slow to anger, abounding in faithful love, and one who relents from sending disaster" (Jonah 4:2). Jonah knew what God would do if he preached. He knew God would be gracious and merciful toward sinners because God had been gracious and merciful to him.

In other words, he resented God for being God. He hated God's merciful and forgiving character when that mercy and forgiveness were aimed at his enemies. He resented God because God's grace to the Ninevites meant the Ninevites were no different from Jonah and the Israelites. He thought he and his people were better than the Ninevites, more deserving of God's grace. Jonah's sin was obvious. He was guilty of ethnocentrism. There was racism and elitism in his heart. In fact, Jonah's actions illustrated the insanity of racism.

The Insanity of Racism

During the early days of slavery in the United States, many slave owners did not want preachers and evangelists coming around their plantation and preaching the gospel of grace to their slaves. Many of these so-called Christian slave owners believed that if their slaves believed the gospel and were saved and baptized, they could no longer hold them in bondage as slaves. The redeemed slaves would now be brothers and sisters in Christ. Therefore, the slave owners would rather keep the gospel from the slaves and, consequently, keep them enslaved rather than rejoice with the slaves in the gospel of God's grace and the inherent freedom that results. For the slave owner, it was a choice between economic riches and eternal riches. When such is the choice, regrettably, eternal riches lose more often than not. Consequently, these so-called Christian slave owners refused the opportunity, like Jonah, to rejoice with those who would rejoice in God. They would rather have slaves and go to hell than have black brothers and sisters to rejoice with on the way to heaven. It's racism. And it's insane.

Furthermore, the insanity of racism causes one to grow numb to it. Jonah's racism and nationalism were so inculcated that he was numb to the insanity of it all. Unfortunately, this is what happens to many of us today. Because of racism we fail to see the glory of God in the diversity of redemption. Because of racism we fail to remember that we are all guilty before the bar of God (Rom. 3:23), and thus the redemption of anyone should be a source of joy for everyone else redeemed. Instead, we regret God's grace for those not like us, as if it means God no longer likes us—like an older sibling jealous of the attention given to a newborn. It sounds crazy because it is.

In the kingdom of God, blessings for one do not mean curses for another. There is no partiality in God (Rom. 2:11). Nor is there a bottom of the well of His grace. The grace of God that abounds for one people group in no way limits or hinders the grace of God available to another. In fact, all are blessed in God when any are blessed in God. This is particularly true when it comes to the blessing of salvation.

The Bible clearly says that God has "from one man" made all the nationalities that inhabit the earth (Acts 17:26). All of us (every nation and every color) are created "from one man."

Another way the Bible says it is that we are all created "from dust" (Eccles. 3:20). Consequently, in God's eyes your lump of dust is not better than my lump of dust, and my lump of dust is not better than your lump of dust. And in fact, if God is pleased to give grace and to save any lump of dust, all other redeemed lumps of dust ought to rejoice! The Bible is clear: white dust is not better than black dust, is not better than red dust, and is not better than brown dust. All dust needs the cleansing power of God's mercy and grace.

Jonah thought Israelite dust was better than Ninevite dust, and it caused him to resent God. Yet, amazingly, God graciously restrained.

God's Restraint

Jonah was insolent. He was disrespectful. He was profane in the face of God. And yet God restrained Himself. Why? Because God is God. And God was going to treat

Jonah, once again, like God treated the Ninevites—with grace. Yet Jonah didn't realize it.

Jonah knew God. He knew God's name. He knew God's character. He knew the self-revelation of God and that God would not and could not act contrary to who God is. This was not the God of Jonah's imagination or even the God of Jonah's own liking. This was the Creator God. This was the God of Abraham, Isaac, and Jacob. This was the God who redeemed Israel out of Egypt and spoke to Moses on Mount Sinai. Jonah knew God and demonstrated this knowledge by quoting the most common description of God found in the Bible. He described God as "a gracious and compassionate God, slow to anger, abounding in faithful love, and one who relents from sending disaster" (Jonah 4:2).

This is how the Bible, over and over again, describes God (Exod. 34:6; Num. 14:18; Neh. 9:17; Pss. 86:15; 103:8; 145:8; Joel 2:13). This is the way God has revealed Himself. He is gracious. He is merciful. He is patient and abounding in steadfast love.

God Is Gracious

For God to be gracious means that "God is good." Being good, God desires good for His creation, especially His people. The psalmist wrote, "You are good, and you do what is good" (Ps. 119:68). Good is God's overall disposition. God is never not good. This is why we say, "God is good all the time, and all the time God is good," because He is. The great promise of one of the most beloved verses in the Bible says that God delights to work all things out for good to those who love Him and are called according to His purpose (Rom. 8:28). No matter what you may think, or what your circumstances may be, or what other people say, the testimony of Scripture over and over again is that God is good. And you especially know this when you come to know Jesus.

Romans 8:32 says, "He [God] did not even spare his own Son [Jesus] but offered him up for us all. How will he not also with him grant us everything?" What does Paul mean by "everything"? All good things. Graciously. Freely. This is the God we worship. This is the God who gave His Son for us. God is good. Grace is good. Jesus is the Son of God, good and full of grace (John 1:14).

God Is Merciful

That God is merciful means that God delights to look beyond our faults and supply our needs. It's not that He doesn't see our faults or our failures. He does. But unlike most people we know, He is willing to see more than our faults. More important, He sees our need—our need for forgiveness, our need for grace, our need for Him. That's mercy. Or put another way—*that's Mama.*

I have an older brother who, for most of his adult life, has been in and out of trouble. He has spent a few years in jail and prison. He has broken the trust of practically all of his brothers and sisters. He has violated his family in many ways. And while others have resolved to have nothing to do with him, my mother takes him back again and again. No matter the circumstance, she always answers the phone. She always has an open door. While others can't see anything but the failure and the faults, his mama looks beyond his faults. His mama looks beyond his failures, and she sees his need—his need for love, his need for acceptance, his need for her. That's what mamas do.

Likewise, God meets our needs. Psalm 46:1 testifies to God's mercy toward us. If you need a safe place, "God is [y]our refuge." If you need power, "God is [y]our . . . strength." If you need help, He is "always found in times of trouble." That's what God does. He looks beyond the faults, and He sees the need. He looks beyond your distresses, shortcomings, and failings and supplies what you need. That is mercy.

God Is Patient

That God is patient means He is slow to anger and self-controlled. He is long-suffering. Nahum 1:3 says, "The LORD is slow to anger but great in power." God has all power, and yet He is patient. Most of the time we are patient because we don't have any choice. Usually, since we cannot do anything about a given situation, we choose to be patient about it. If we have power to change a situation, we are often not so patient. Not so with God! If something is not the way He desires it to be, He could change it at any moment. He doesn't have to wait. Amazingly, He has all power, and yet He is patient and slow to anger.

Let's be clear: God does get angry (see Num. 12:9; Deut. 6:15; Hab. 3:12). However, unlike you and me, His anger never gets the best of Him. He never acts in a way that He later regrets. He never does or says anything for which He later has to apologize. Even in His anger He is patient. Psalm 78:38 speaks of God's dealing with His wayward and rebellious people:

> Yet he was compassionate;
> he atoned for their iniquity
> and did not destroy them.
> He often turned his anger aside
> and did not unleash all his wrath.

Time after time He restrained His anger and did not stir up His full wrath. I find these words humbling and most assuring: "time after time." I don't know about you, but that's my life every day. Every day, time after time, God is merciful and patient with me. As angry as I get and as impatient as I am, time after time God is patient. Time after time, after time, after time, He restrains His anger.

All Jonah did was charge God with being God, and in doing so he revealed the darkness of his own heart. He did not falsely accuse God; he disdained God for who God is. He showed contempt for God. He hated God's compassion. He resented God's kindness. He decried God's patience. He regretted God's mercy. But let's not be too quick to condemn Jonah; we must admit that these same sentiments are too often found in you and me.

Jonah forgot that God was gracious to him. Jonah forgot that God was kind to him. Jonah forgot that God was merciful and patient with him. Ironically, we love God for being patient with us, but we are not always enthused when He is patient with a spouse or patient with our children. We're not so enthused when He is patient with a coworker, a supervisor, a neighbor, a brother, or a sister. We want God to be angry with those who sin against us, but we are not always so enthused when His anger is against our sin. When God is merciful to those who show us no mercy, we easily find ourselves despising God for being God. We grow impatient because we perceive He is taking too long to change other people. He's taking too long to make them "what I want them to be." We resent Him for giving others space to repent. So like Jonah, many of us grow angry and grow resentful because God doesn't do what we want Him to do, when we want Him to do it. We must admit this is sin.

Jonah was in sin. Resenting God is sin. Accusing God of wrong is sin. Not trusting God's will and submitting to His ways is sin. And yet the only known cure for sin is found in the good, gracious, patient, merciful character of God.

Consider just how gracious God has been in redeeming you. Consider how patient He has been in forgiving you. Consider how merciful He has been in looking past your failures and, rather than condemning you (Rom. 8:1), supplying you with all things good in Christ Jesus.

When you consider again the goodness and the grace of God, the patience and the kindness of God, the love and the mercy of God, you find yourself faced with the same question God asked Jonah: "Is it right for you to be angry?" (Jonah 4:4). Or, to put it another way, "Have you any reason to complain?"

Look again at the grace of God despite the depths of your sin. See the goodness of God in your life and all the blessings He delights to graciously bestow on you, though you don't deserve any of them. Then honestly ask yourself the question, "Do I really have a reason to complain?"

Consider the church and the community of the saints and that God has granted you the privilege of being named among His people. Consider the privilege of singing the songs of Zion, of hearing God's Word read, of the prayers of the saints prayed. Consider that despite your waywardness and disobedience, God has welcomed you into the place where He is pleased to dwell. Do you really have a reason to complain?

See again Jesus upon the cross. Despised and rejected. Wounded and bruised. The sinless Son of God taking the wrath you and I deserve. Purchasing our redemption with His precious blood. And ask yourself the question, "Is it right for me to be angry?"

Consider the words of the song, "I Won't Complain":

> *I see the depths of the Father's love*
> *I won't complain.*
> *His mercy came down from up above,*
> *I won't complain.*
> *When all my sin He has owned*
> *The great extent to which He's gone*
> *No greater love has anyone known*
> *I won't complain*

From the wounds in His nail-scarred hands
I won't complain.
Upon His head a thorn-filled band
I won't complain.
With his body broken and blood shed
Not a displeasing word He said
All for me He bowed his head
I won't complain

O, let us praise His holy name!
The Lord is good, yes He is
And true to all his promises
Why should I complain?

I know He's risen from the grave
I won't complain
I know He has the power to save I won't
    complain
His Holy Spirit with me abide
The risen Christ at the Father's side
In Him I have eternal life
No, no I won't complain.[28]

Jonah had no reason to complain. Because of Jesus neither do I. Neither do you.

Our Big God
Jonah 4:5–11

———

Jonah left the city and found a place east of it. He made himself a shelter there and sat in its shade to see what would happen to the city. Then the LORD God appointed a plant, and it grew over Jonah to provide shade for his head to rescue him from his trouble. Jonah was greatly pleased with the plant. When dawn came the next day, God appointed a worm that attacked the plant, and it withered.

As the sun was rising, God appointed a scorching east wind. The sun beat down on Jonah's head so much that he almost fainted, and he wanted to die. He said, "It's better for me to die than to live."

Then God asked Jonah, "Is it right for you to be angry about the plant?"

"Yes, it's right!" he replied. "I'm angry enough to die!"

So the LORD said, "You cared about the plant, which you did not labor over and did not grow. It appeared in a night and perished in a night. But may I not care about the great city of Nineveh, which has more than a hundred and twenty thousand people who cannot distinguish between their right and their left, as well as many animals?"

Winter is a great teacher. I grew up in Michigan, and there I learned many valuable lessons during the winter seasons. I learned that snow accumulates fast. Many folks don't understand that because snow typically falls so slow and it looks so pretty and innocent. Yet in a place like Michigan, you quickly learn that it accumulates fast, and before you know it, you are snowed in.

The second thing I learned is that nobody can drive on ice. No matter what those from Northern states may say or how much they mock their Southern state friends for not being able to navigate ice-covered roads, up North they're not driving on ice either. Nobody can drive on ice.

The third thing I learned growing up in Michigan is that cold is nothing to play with. One minute you think you're playing in it, and the next minute it's all over you. Many people have found themselves in dire situations in a moment's notice because they did not carefully consider how cold it was. Cold is nothing to play with.

Yes, winter is a valuable teacher, and it taught me many lessons. For the Christian, learning lessons is just part of life. The Christian is a learner.

That's what it means to be a disciple. A disciple is a learner who is determined to learn from the Lord every day. The faithful Christian is a learner who is willing to be challenged, corrected, and, if necessary, disciplined.

The Christian life is a life of submitting to the truth and, when confronted with it, willingly embracing it. It's what Christians do: we learn. The Bible has names for those who do not care to learn: *mockers* and *fools*. According to the Scriptures:

> Don't rebuke a mocker, or he will hate you;
> rebuke the wise, and he will love you. (Prov. 9:8)

> A wise son responds to his father's discipline,
> but a mocker doesn't listen to rebuke. (Prov. 13:1)

> A mocker doesn't love one who corrects him;
> he will not consult the wise. (Prov. 15:12)

The scoffer does not want to be corrected and, in fact, refuses to be. He fights against reproof and is unwilling to turn from his foolish ways. He is not a learner and, therefore, is not a disciple. To be a disciple is to be willing to accept reproof and correction, and thereby grow in the knowledge and understanding of Jesus Christ. Admittedly, we are all scoffers until we are changed by the grace and mercy of God.

The prophecy of Jonah is the life lesson of a scoffer turned disciple, who learned the lesson taught to him by

God. Jonah was a scoffer. The prophecy of Jonah is a lesson learned. It was a lesson to Jonah. It was a lesson to the nation of Israel. It is a lesson to us all. The lesson is clear and clearly taught in the final scene of the prophecy; namely, *our God is big*. Jonah teaches us that we serve a big God.

God Is Big

To be a Christian is to have a theology of a big God. To say, "God is big," is simply to say that *God is sovereign*—that God sees all things, knows all things, controls all things, and ordains all things.

If you go into your average Christian bookstore and begin to browse the best-seller list, what you see most are books that have at their center big men and big women. But the Bible is not about big men and big women. The Bible is about a big God. And in fact, you can't have a big God *and* a big you. This is what Jonah teaches us. God is big; Jonah, you're not.

Jonah is a prophecy of all things great. If you go back and read it again from chapter 1, you will be amazed at how often you are struck with the idea of greatness. Nineveh is called a *great* city. God sent a *great* wind, which caused a *great* storm. Jonah is thrown overboard and swallowed by a *great* fish. As a result, there is *great* repentance and *great* revival.

The prophecy of Jonah contains many great things. Yet nothing in the prophecy of Jonah is greater than God. Nothing is greater than God and His mission.

Our lives are consumed with things we believe are big deals. Big ideas. Big problems. Big questions. Big answers. Big people. Jonah thought he was big. He thought his problems and his situation were big. Yet as chapter 4 closes, we learn that God was showing Jonah what big really is. Big is God. Or better yet, God is big.

The lesson for the disciple to learn is that God is bigger than your circumstances. God is bigger than your attitude. God is bigger than your concerns.

God Is Bigger than Your Circumstances

By the time we reach the concluding section of chapter 4, Jonah had resolved that all was lost. He was disgruntled. He felt alone and abandoned by God. He believed God had ignored him and dismissed any and all of his complaints. Essentially, he said to God, "I'm done. Forget it, Lord. I'm taking my ball and I'm going home." He was overwhelmed by his circumstances, and he just wanted to be left alone. That's what he said: "Lord, leave me alone. I'm going to build this little hut, sit under this tree, watch what goes on, and hope to die. Leave me alone!" These sentiments sound too familiar.

When things don't go our way, often the first thing we want to do is run away. We want to be left alone. We clam up, we shut up, and we shut people out.

In our home, when our kids were young, whenever one of them said, "Leave me alone," we'd say, "Oh no, you don't want to be left alone. We can arrange for you to be left alone if you really want to be left alone, but we guarantee, you really don't want to be left alone."

Nevertheless, even if we don't verbalize it, we show it. I see it happen at church. I see it happen in relationships. Something doesn't go our way, or a decision is made contrary to our opinion, or the program doesn't progress the way we planned, and we let our feet do the talking. With our actions we say, "I'm done. I'm taking my ball and going home. Leave me alone."

This was Jonah. We have all been there, but here's the thing: God won't leave you alone. If you belong to Him and are the recipient of His saving grace and love, He won't leave you alone. He knows what you really need is not to be left alone. Rather, you need to be reminded of the fact that He is bigger than your circumstances. He didn't leave Jonah alone. Instead, what God did was remind Jonah that God controlled Jonah's circumstances.

God Controlled Jonah's Circumstances

God was in control. Where Jonah decided to build a tent for himself, God created shade (Jonah 4:5-6). Jonah was not called to build shade for Jonah—that was God's responsibility. To demonstrate His control, God made another appointment with Jonah. The Bible says, "God appointed a plant" (v. 6). Like He had appointed a fish and appointed a wind, God appointed a plant. The plant was made to come up "over Jonah to provide shade for his head to rescue him from his trouble." And yet the plant was appointed not just to provide shade for Jonah but, more important, to show Jonah who was in control. God was.

Graciously, however it may look, we are never left alone. Our circumstances are never out of control. In fact, they are never really in our control. Our lives are in the hands of our almighty and benevolent God. God governs our circumstances. God provides the shade. The Bible says, "The LORD protects you; the LORD is a shelter right by your side. The sun will not strike you by day or the moon by night" (Ps. 121:5-6). God provided comfort, even for His rebellious child!

Don't get it twisted. Any comfort in this life comes from God. You know what Jonah did? Jonah toiled to bring himself comfort, and yet the comfort that he actually did have was a comfort that came through the grace and mercy and the goodness of God. Oh, how often we believe we are actually providing for ourselves.

At times I have to travel out of town for ministry. When I leave my family, one of my prayers is, "Lord, protect my family while I'm gone." While I mean it in all sincerity, the foolishness in that prayer is the assumption that God somehow is not protecting my family while I'm there. The fact of the matter is that any protection, any covering, any shade, any comfort that we have, whether I'm here or I'm gone, is because of the mercy and the goodness of God. He provides the shade. He provides the covering.

This plant that God appointed for Jonah sprouted up and grew over him. It provided a shade so that the sun didn't beat him by day or the moon by night. And notice Jonah's response: "Jonah was greatly pleased with the plant" (Jonah 4:6). Unfortunately, Jonah found his gladness in the comfort rather than in the Comforter. This is crucial to understand.

Jonah was glad for the plant, but he wasn't willing to acknowledge the Planter. Jonah was full of joy. The plant had grown up overnight and had covered him better than anything he could do with his own hands. He was exceedingly glad and filled with joy for the plant.

But the plant should not have been Jonah's source of joy. He should have been glad in the Planter. Jonah was exceedingly glad and rejoiced in the plant because like us, he was prone to be more thankful for the blessing than the blessing Giver.

We must be careful about getting too excited about our comforts. We should get excited about the Comforter. This is what God desires because this is where true, lasting joy is found.

The Bible tells us over and over again that the Lord is our joy. He is not only our shade but also our everlasting joy. True, lasting joy is not found in things. True joy is found in God.

Joy is in the power of God.

> The LORD had done great things for us; we were joyful. (Ps. 126:3)

Joy is in the presence of God.

> In your presence is abundant joy; at your right hand are eternal pleasures. (Ps. 16:11)

Joy is in the praise of God.

> I will offer sacrifices in his tent with shouts of joy. I will sing and make music to the LORD." (Ps. 27:6)

Joy is found in the person of God.

> Then I will come to the altar of God, to
> God, my greatest joy. (Ps. 43:4)

God is our joy! God is the source of our comfort and contentment. Jesus is not only in us, our hope of glory (Col. 1:27), but Jesus is in us, our hope—the center of our joy.

God taught Jonah that God is in control. God's control of all things is not a cause of concern or distress. On the contrary, it should be the source of comfort and joy. It's the lesson God teaches all His disciples. God was in control of Jonah's circumstances, and therefore, God changed Jonah's circumstances.

God Changed Jonah's Circumstances

Jonah failed to recognize God as his comfort in all things; therefore, God changed things for Jonah. God had another appointment for Jonah. In fact, He had two more appointments for Jonah. Remember, when God makes appointments, you don't cancel and you don't reschedule. You can't call Him up and say, "Hey God, I'm running late. Can we reschedule?" You don't come late. You don't reschedule. God's appointments are always kept on time. And God had two more appointments for Jonah. The Bible says:

When dawn came the next day, God *appointed* a worm that attacked the plant, and it withered.

As the sun was rising, God *appointed* a scorching east wind. The sun beat down on Jonah's head so much that he almost fainted, and he wanted to die. He said, "It's better for me to die than to live." (4:7–8, emphasis added)

God appointed a worm to eat the plant, and then He appointed the wind and the sun to beat down on Jonah. God took Jonah's comforts. Jonah had to learn who was in control. He had to learn from whom his help and comforts came. He had to learn the source of his satisfaction.

God won't allow us to find lasting satisfaction outside of Him. In fact, God will take away comforts and blessings, even the ones He gives, if those comforts and blessings keep us from Him. This may sound harsh. After all, wouldn't a loving God want us to be comforted? He does want us to be comforted, but because we were made for Him, He knows we cannot be truly comforted in anything but Him. Thus, in His grace, He will not allow us to find satisfaction apart from Him.

This is a lesson God teaches to all, even the apostle Paul.

Paul had wonderful blessings from God. In fact, he had revelations and insights into things perhaps none on earth has ever seen (2 Cor. 12:1-4). These insights and revelations must have been a wonderful privilege and incalculable blessing to the soul of Paul. And yet God was also careful to assure that Paul didn't make more of the blessings than the blessing Giver. Accordingly, Paul wrote:

> Because of the surpassing greatness of the revelations, for this reason, to keep me from exalting myself, there was given me a thorn in the flesh, a messenger of Satan to torment me—to keep me from exalting myself! Concerning this I implored the Lord three times that it might leave me. And He has said to me, "My grace is sufficient for you, for power is perfected in weakness." Most gladly, therefore, I will rather boast about my weaknesses, so that the power of Christ may dwell in me. (2 Cor. 12:7-9 NASB)

Paul recognized that the affliction was from God, just as the revelations were. Consequently, Paul could rejoice even in the affliction because the source of his comfort was not the plant but the Planter—not the comforts of this life but the Comforter. Jonah, unfortunately, did not.

Rather than doing what Paul did and finding the joy of the Lord in the midst of trial, Jonah got an attitude. Consequently, God not only showed Jonah that He is bigger than Jonah's circumstances, but He also showed Jonah that He is bigger than his attitude.

God Is Bigger than Your Attitude

Jonah had an attitude of discontentment. He was discontent with life. He grew discontent with his situation and God's continued mercy toward Nineveh. God withdrew the plant, and Jonah withdrew into discontentment, dissatisfaction, and discouragement. He thought his circumstances were unredeemable and irreconcilable. He wanted to give it all up and pleaded to die, saying, "It's better for me to die than to live" (Jonah 4:8).

Discontentment is the attitude of dissatisfaction. It is a longing for change and a chronic unhappiness until that change comes. Because God is sovereign over our circumstances, discontentment is being dissatisfied with God, even longing for something or someone more than God. It is an attitude and a malady that is foremost in our time.

If we know anything to be true about the human condition, particularly in our culture, it is that human hearts are discontent. People make millions and billions of dollars playing on the fact that you and I are discontent. Every year companies pay millions of dollars for a few seconds of television advertisement during the Super Bowl, preying on our discontentment and showing us how desperately we need their product to be happy.

Journalist and author Gregg Easterbrook has written a book entitled *The Progress Paradox: How Life Gets Better While People Feel Worse.* (What an insightful title.) The quality of our lives improves almost every day. People live longer. A generation ago few would have dreamed of the advances in health today. Advances in technology are making life easier for us by the minute. There are advances in information and communication, to the point that you can click a button and instantly find out what is happening in some of the remotest parts of the world. With one click from my home in Atlanta, Georgia, I can watch a live video of life in Antarctica. It is amazing!

Still, with all the advances in technology, information, entertainment, health, and communications, the happiness and contentment quotients continue to go down. Honestly, the world has sold us a bag of lies. The world has told us that people and things make us happy, and we have believed it. We convince ourselves that if we can just get a little more money, or get out of school, or get a different job, or find that soul mate, or have a baby, or go on vacation, or finally retire, we would finally be happy.

These are the lies the enemy and the world adeptly sell to us every day. These are the lies that, unfortunately, many Christians buy into (literally). Though most of us would deny we have bought in, an honest survey of our lives says otherwise. Too much of our joy and satisfaction fluctuates with the things and people we have or don't have in our lives. This world is fleeting and fickle, and so, too, are all satisfaction, happiness, and contentment that are too closely tied to it.

God wanted Jonah to learn the lesson of all lessons—the lesson of *the secret of true contentment*. It's a lesson God desires to teach all of His disciples. Remember, it's the lesson he taught our brother Paul, who wrote:

> I don't say this out of need, for I have learned to be content in whatever circumstances I find myself. I know both how to make do with little, and I know how to make do with a lot. In any and all circumstances I have learned the secret of being content—whether well fed or hungry, whether in abundance or in need. [And here is the secret.] *I am able to*

> *do all things through him [Christ] who strengthens*
> *me.* (Phil. 4:11–13, emphasis added)

That's the secret! Then again, it really is not a secret, is it? It's right there plainly stated in the Bible for us. It is not written in secret code. You don't have to decipher it. You don't have to use numerology or consult the stars or mediums. There really is no secret. *Christ is the key to contentment.*

There is no more important lesson to learn than the lesson of being satisfied in Jesus. Where is that person who is truly content? Where is that man or woman who is truly satisfied in Jesus? That man or woman is unique. He is untouchable, unflappable, and unstoppable.

Untouchable

The content woman or man is untouchable. The enemy will come to him and find nothing. The world will tempt him over and over again and come up empty. To be truly content in Jesus would be a satisfaction impenetrable by this world. Untouchable.

Unflappable

The storms of life will come. It could be clear and sunny one day and cloudy and overcast the next. The stock market could go through the roof one day and crash the next. Yet the content man or woman would be unflappable. You would see them every day and the joy of the Lord would not have waned. He would walk into church every Sunday because for him nothing matters more than Jesus. Unflappable.

Unstoppable

God would send the content man or woman on mission, and He cannot be stopped. Nothing could stop him from praising God. Nothing could stop him from serving God. He'd never take his ball and go home. He'd stay on mission until the Lord's return. Unstoppable.

Have you ever wondered what drove the apostle Paul? I believe it was his satisfaction in Jesus! He realized all he had and needed was in Christ Jesus. Christ was enough. That's why Paul was untouchable. That's why he was unflappable. That's why he was unstoppable.

What about you? Life changes when you realize and trust that God is bigger. He is bigger than your circumstances, attitudes, and discontentment. To it all, God says, "Put it away. I'm greater than all that. And in Me you can be too."

Unfortunately, Jonah was not only discontented; Jonah was angry. Like Job's wife, Jonah had anger issues and consequently wanted to "curse God and die" (Job 2:9; see Jonah 4:9). Why was he angry? He was angry for the same reason you and I get angry. We get angry when we can't have our way. So did Jonah.

From the youngest child to the oldest adult, an attitude of anger is usually the result of our not getting things the way we want them to be. Anger creates an atmosphere of distrust or—even worse—self-trust. Dan Doriani makes the point, "Anger not only makes it difficult to get along with other people, anger makes it difficult to get along with God."[29] Still Jonah's anger did not stress God. Jonah would have to learn, as we all do, that our anger does not accomplish the righteousness of God (James 1:20). Only Christ can do that!

God Is Bigger than Your Concerns

Because he had an attitude, Jonah believed he had big concerns. God said to Jonah: "You cared about the plant, which you did not labor over and did not grow" (Jonah 4:10). Jonah was concerned about the plant. God may have been concerned about the plant too, but His greater concern was Jonah. His greater concern was Nineveh.

Jonah's concern for the plant revealed Jonah's real concern—himself. You may be tempted to think it noble or sweet that Jonah was concerned for the plant. No, Jonah was not concerned for the plant as much as he was concerned for himself. His concern for the plant only existed insofar as the plant provided something he desired. Jonah was concerned that he would no longer have the shade. He was concerned for his own comfort.

But while Jonah was concerned for himself and his loss of shade, God was concerned for the lost in the city of Nineveh. And here is the great difference. Jonah was concerned for the plant because of what he might lose. God was concerned for Nineveh because of what they might lose—namely, God.

Jonah's concern, as we've seen, was only for Israel. God's concern and His mission are much bigger than that. His mission and concern are for the nations. God's concerns are bigger than your concerns. God says, "Yes, I'm concerned for Israel. But I'm concerned for the nations too. I'm concerned that My glory be known not only in Israel but throughout all creation." That's big.

It's big when you understand that God has this big agenda. It helps to understand that while God is concerned about your concerns, He also has greater, grander concerns of which you and I, like Jonah, play a part. He is a big God with a big agenda. He's bringing His kingdom to bear upon the world. He's changing the face of His people. He will have His name be great in Israel. But He will not stop there. Israel was first but not last (Rom. 1:16). The nations will show forth the glory of God in greater splendor than even Israel. We will do it together with Israel in Jesus Christ, God's Son. And the glory of this house will be greater than the former one (Hag. 2:9; Eph. 2:15).

This is what Jonah didn't understand, just as this was the lesson the older brother had to learn. In the parable of the prodigal son, when the older brother grumbled and became angry and discontent, the father said, "Son, . . . you are always with me, and everything I have is yours. But we had to celebrate and rejoice, because this brother of yours was dead and is alive again; he was lost and is found" (Luke 15:31–32).

That the nations would be coming to the knowledge of the glory of God should have caused Jonah to rejoice. That God is still saving people from every tribe, tongue, and nation in Jesus should call all of His people to rejoice. This is the bigness of God. This is the greatness of God's love in the gospel of Jesus Christ: "For God loved the world [the nations] in this way: He gave his one and only Son, so that everyone [in the world, in the nations] who believes in him will not perish but have eternal life" (John 3:16).

Jonah probably would have hated John 3:16. But it is the most beloved verse in the Bible. Every Sunday morning all around the world, the redeemed of God are gathered from every tribe, tongue, and nation giving testimony to the beauty and glory of John 3:16. That's big! That's great! That's God!

When I was a little boy, every Sunday morning as we prepared for church, we watched Oral Roberts on television. The best part of the show was when the Oral Roberts singers would come out and sing the opening song: "God Is Greater." The whole song is about the glory and greatness of God.

That's what Jonah had to learn. That's what Jonah's life teaches us today. God is great and so is His grace. Therefore, trust that "the one who is in you is greater than the one who is in the world" (1 John 4:4). Trust that greater is grace than all your sin (see Rom. 5:20). Trust in God. He is great and greatly to be praised.

Mercy Came Running

One of the great human stories of history is the life of John Newton. The eighteenth-century English pastor is best known as the author of the hymn "Amazing Grace." The words of the song are not just poetry but autobiographical verse. Prior to being saved, Newton was a sailor, a blasphemer, and a scoffer of God. He not only scoffed at God but also openly mocked those who dared to believe in God. He eventually became a slave ship captain and, by his own account, was one of the best (or worst) of all slavers. And yet to this man, who by his own account was the vilest of sinners, the mercy of God came running.

In a self-description, John Newton wrote theses words as his epitaph:

> John Newton. Clerk. Once an infidel and libertine—a servant of slaves in Africa—was by the rich mercy of our Lord and Savior Jesus Christ, preserved, restored, pardoned and appointed to preach the faith he had long labored to destroy.

John Newton discovered to his amazement that the God whom he had mocked and blasphemed was actually a God of mercy and grace. Mercy came running to John Newton when he least deserved it. It likewise came to Jonah. It likewise comes to us.

Jonah is the most human of stories. It is the everyman and every woman experience with God. It is the story of rebellious sinners running from God and God surprisingly responding in merciful pursuit. It is the old story of the sinner saying no and thumbing his nose at God, and yet God in mercy still saying yes and working all things together for the sinner's good.

Who hasn't resisted God's will? Who hasn't run from God or tried to circumvent God's commands? Jonah is the everyman's prophet. More times than I care to recount, I have found myself rationalizing away God's will for the pursuit of my own. And whether storm or fish, God ordains the means of bringing me back to Him—back to life.

No, I haven't been swallowed up by a fish—and I am pretty confident you haven't either. But perhaps you were swallowed up by a bad relationship. Perhaps you were swallowed by drug or alcohol dependence. Perhaps you were swallowed by an unwanted pregnancy, sexual harassment, or abuse. Perhaps you were swallowed by an illness, the loss of a loved one, loneliness, or shame. And, like Jonah, you were cast down into the depths of darkness, even into a grave of sorts. You might have thought your life was over, never again to be used by God. Indeed, the great fish would have consumed you except that you realized God ordained that fish, or trial, not for your death but for your life. He brought you low to save you.

That fish was appointed by God as a means of delivering you and teaching you the greatest truth of all—namely, "Salvation is of the Lord." This was the joy and comfort of Jonah, and the joy and comfort of all those who know that Jonah's God saves.

My testimony is a simple one. I sought to live my life seeking pleasure and fulfillment in all the world had to offer. Popularity, pleasure, and the pursuit of worldly possessions, however, left me lonely. I was the life of the party—until the party was over. I went from job to job and relationship to relationship, yet nothing lasted or gave me the contentment my heart so longed to have.

I was raised in a small rural church and came to know the Lord as a young boy in Sunday school. But as I grew, salvation became a box to be checked, not a life to be lived.

Then one lonely evening I felt the Spirit of the Lord ask me, "*What are you doing about your sin?*" I was twenty-one years old. I knew Christ had died for my sin, and yet my sin was still burdening me and causing pain to others. That evening the Holy Spirit reminded me that Christ died for my sin, and by holding on to it, I was forsaking the joy that was inherently mine. In other words, I never knew the joy of my salvation until I knew the misery of my sin. I prayed again for the Lord to save me. That day God brought me to see the misery of my sin, and I knew that I, like the apostle Paul, had received God's mercy (1 Tim. 1:13). Mercy came running to me and brought joy and grace with him.

If the prophecy of Jonah teaches us anything, it teaches us mercy doesn't run after the righteous, but like Jesus (Mark 2:17), mercy comes running to sinners. Like it did with John Newton, mercy runs after the blasphemers, mockers, arrogant, lustful, and idolatrous. It pursues the poor, the helpless, the needy, the captive, the rejected, the shameful, and the despised. Mercy met the woman at the well (John 4). Mercy called out to Zaccheaus (Luke 19:1–10). Mercy rescued the woman caught in adultery (John 8). Mercy sought out Peter, and the other disciples, after Peter's betrayal (Mark 16:7). Mercy ran down Paul on the road to Damascus (Acts 9). And even now mercy comes running after you and me. It is mercy we need and, therefore, mercy we receive—undeserved, unearned, life-changing mercy.

God is not passive in His pursuit of us. He calls and then He comes after those He calls. He comes with goodness and mercy. Years ago Philips, Craig and Dean summed it up well in song:

> *Mercy came running*
> *Like a prisoner set free,*
> *Past all my failures to the point of my need.*
> *When the sin that I carried*
> *Was all I could see*
> *And when I could not reach mercy,*
> *Mercy came running to me.*[30]

Wherever you are today, you can stop running. God's mercy is coming, bringing God's grace and forgiveness with Him.

Study Questions

Chapter 1

1. What do you think of when you picture prophets in the Old Testament? How do you picture Jonah?

2. Jonah fled from the will of God. What does fleeing God's will look like in your life?

3. Jonah quickly experienced the character and attributes of God. What are those attributes?

4. What does it mean for God to be omnipresent?

5. What does it mean for God to be omnipotent?

6. What does it mean for God to be omniscient?

7. What role should each of these attributes play in our daily lives?

Chapter 2

1. What is the providence of God?

2. What are some of the clear demonstrations of God's providence in the book of Jonah?

3. What is the goal of God's providence?

4. What is the relationship between providence and grace?

5. How has God's providence looked in your life?

6. Have you ever experienced anything like the words written in "The Hound of Heaven"?

7. What makes providence a sweet and comforting truth for believers in Christ?

Chapter 3

1. How do you feel about being on time for an appointment? Does it bother you when people show up late or cancel on you?

2. "The LORD appointed a great fish to swallow Jonah" (Jonah 1:17). What strikes you about God's appointment in this sentence?

3. What is most remarkable to you about the means God appoints to accomplish His will in Jonah's life and in yours?

4. Do you find it difficult waiting for God's appointed time?

5. How would you encourage someone who appears to be in God's waiting room?

6. Why does it please God when we cry to Him out of the depths of our misery?

Chapter 4

1. What is repentance?

2. Jesus, John the Baptist, and the apostles preached repentance from sin. What role should repentance play in our preaching and evangelism today?

3. How does Jonah acknowledge his sin?

4. What does is sound like when you acknowledge your sin?

5. What is mercy?

6. "Salvation belongs to the LORD" (Ps. 3:8). How does the Bible make this clear? How is this a comfort and joy for repentant sinners?

Chapter 5

1. What is redemption?

2. "Everyone deserves a second chance." Is this true? Why or why not?

3. Have you ever felt that God has given you a second chance? If so, did His commands change the second time around?

4. Why is it difficult to understand God's relenting or changing His mind?

5. What does the Bible mean when it says God changed His mind?

6. Why is it good to remember that God pursues us for good and not harm, for grace and not condemnation?

Chapter 6

1. Jonah's resentment of God's grace was rooted in pride, which produced an elitism and racism. How so?

2. In what ways are we all susceptible to racist and elitist thinking and feelings?

3. How is racism a manifestation of insanity? How do we guard against it?

4. God's restraint is rooted in His character. What virtues does this chapter teach us are found in God?

5. How are you impacted by the fact that God is gracious, merciful, and patient?

6. Have you ever resented God's grace, mercy, and patience?

Chapter 7

1. Was school a good, bad, or indifferent time for you?

2. God took Jonah to school. Has God ever schooled you on life? What did you learn?

3. Jonah learned that God is big. What does "God is big" mean?

4. Why is it good to know God is bigger than your circumstances?

5. Discontentment is a common spiritual illness. What is the cure for discontentment?

6. The greatness of God is the greatness of grace for the nations. What are the biblical implications of the gospel's going to the Ninevites?

7. What difference has it made for the gospel to come to you?

Notes

1. Fanny J. Crosby, "He Hideth My Soul."

2. A. W. Tozer, *Whatever Happened to Worship?* (Wingspread; revised edition, 2012).

3. Nicholson, D. H. S., and A. H. E. Lee, eds. *The Oxford Book of English Mystical Verse* (Oxford: The Clarendon Press, 1917); Bartleby. com, 2000, www.bartleby.com/236/.

4. Heidelberg Catechism, Lord's Day 10, Question 27.

5. Wilhelmus à Brakel, *The Christian's Reasonable Service* (Grand Rapids, MI: Reformation Heritage Books, 1992), 332.

6. Isaac Watts, "I Sing the Mighty Power of God."

7. William Cowyer, "God Moves in a Mysterious Way," 1774.

8. Ibid.

9. Richard Smallwood, "What He's Done for Me," 1992.

10. *The Psalms and Hymns of Isaac Watts* (Morgan, PA: Soli Deo Publications, 1997), 239.

11. Henry J. Zelley, "He Brought Me Out," 1898.

12. Joseph Hart, "Come Ye Sinners, Poor, and Needy."

13. Wayne Grudem, *Systematic Theology* (Grand Rapids, MI: Zondervan, 1994), 713.

14. Westminster Shorter Catechism, Question 87.

15. Thomas Carlisle, *You! Jonah!* (Grand Rapids, MI: Eerdmans, 1968), 21.

16. William R. Newell, "At Calvary."

17. Timothy Keller, *Counterfeit Gods: The Empty Promises of Money, Sex, and Power, and the Only Hope That Matters* (New York, NY: Dutton, 2009), xv.

18. Ibid.

19. Ibid, xvii.

20. Horatio Bonar, "I Heard the Voice of Jesus Say."

21. William Banks, *Jonah: the Reluctant Prophet* (Chicago: Moody, 1996), 72.

22. Writer is Doris Akers.

23. O. Palmer Robertson, *Jonah: A Study in Compassion* (Edinburgh: Banner of Truth, 1990), 42.

24. Fanny J. Crosby, "Redeemed, How I Love to Proclaim It."

25. Nicholson and Lee, eds. *The Oxford Book of English Mystical Verse.*

26. Michael Card, "Hound of Heaven" (Benson Music, 2009).

27. Allen C. Myers, ed., *The Eerdmans Bible Dictionary* (Grand Rapids, MI: Eerdmans, 1987), 102.

28. Anthony J. Carter, "I Won't Complain" (East Point Music, 2014).

29. Dan Doriani sermon, "Hearing to Obey," June 19, 2011, James 1:19–25.

30. Don Koch, Dave Clark, Dan Dean, "Mercy Came Running" (Warner/Chappell Music, Inc., Universal Music Publishing Group, Capitol Christian Music Group, 1995).